Dedicated to Ila Davis,
who left my life too soon,
a dear friend who died in a
tragic boating accident
while living life on her own terms—
Living by Spirit Alone.

Contents

LIVING BY
YOUR BRUSH
ALONE

Margaret Mullen-Hart
516 East Second St.
Fairmount, Indiana
46928

Edna Wagner Piersol

NORTH LIGHT BOOKS

Cincinnati, Ohio

Living by Your Brush Alone. Copyright © 1989 by Edna
Wagner Piersol. Printed and bound in United States of
America. All rights reserved. No part of this book may be
reproduced in any form or by any electronic or mechanical
means including information storage and retrieval systems
without permission in writing from the publisher, except
by a reviewer, who may quote brief passages in a review.
Published by North Light Books, an imprint of F&W Publi-
cations, Inc., 1507 Dana Avenue, Cincinnati, Ohio 45207.
First edition.

93 92 91 90 89   5 4 3 2 1

Library of Congress Cataloging in Publication Data

Piersol, Edna Wagner.
    Living by your brush alone/Edna Wagner Piersol.
        p. cm.
    Rev. ed. of: An artist's guide to living by your brush alone.
1983.
    Includes index.
    ISBN 0-89134-294-X
    1. Art—Vocational guidance. I. Piersol, Edna Wagner.
Artist's guide to living by your brush alone. II. Title.
N8350.P54   1989   89-3115
706'.8—dc19   CIP

Edited by Linda Sanders

Introduction

It is easy to become a starving artist. It comes naturally—no special skills required. But learning how to survive supported only by your paintbrush, while remaining true to your own ideals of art—that is another thing. Don't think it will ruin you as an artist to make money by working at it. More likely, the process will improve your approach to life and, in turn, will make you a better artist.

Take a look at the Old Masters. What did they have to do to survive as artists? Was Michelangelo allowed to be himself? Not really. He was trained in Ghirlandaio's workshop and Bertoldo's school in the Medici gardens. No doubt, he had to abandon work he wanted to do in order to meet the demands of the day. Yet he was so independent in his assigned tasks that his talent came through as strongly as if he had been allowed to follow his own dictates.

There are many books these days telling us how to paint, but what about how to *live* as artists? How do we survive in the real world and remain free to paint and create?

One way is to realize that we *can* do it. We can find ways to make a living as artists in a freer way than was open even to artists like Michelangelo. Usually we can live exactly as we want without sacrificing our standards. So don't throw up your hands sighing, My God, she wants me to worry about selling my work. I don't care if you ever sell. But don't complain if you then have to trudge through life, working at a job you don't like when you could be living, happily, by your brush alone . . . creating pictures every day of your joyous life.

CHAPTER ONE

Courage to Live by Your Brush Alone

Once when I was standing before a group of artists, lecturing on the merits of self-assurance, I watched the facial expressions of those assembled in front of me. The looks flew back questioning: How did you have the courage to take off and begin to live by your brush alone? The truth is, I didn't. But I needed to live that way so strongly that courage didn't figure in my thinking. Experience taught me many things—things that can benefit every artist.

When you are trying to live on your own, your worst enemy is yourself. For one thing, we all tend to put ourselves into categories. What we say we are, we become. If we call ourselves unsuccessful artists, that's what we will be. When we say we can't do something, we usually mean we are afraid to try. There is one sure way to never fail: never try.

I have learned to ignore fear. I've told myself I am a successful artist because I am a good artist. Try it. If you want to live by your brush alone, it is possible.

What do you think would happen if you stopped someone on the street and asked if he'd like to own a fine painting? I doubt that anyone would say no. Few other products garner a more positive response. Your only problem is to get a painting to each person who wants one at a price he can afford—and a price that will also earn you a little profit.

Choosing Your League

It was nearly two years after I began living solely from my painting that I finally began to believe I was *doing* it. It was too good to be true—living the way I wanted without fear of tomorrow. Although I joke about it, a starving artist I am not. How did this come about? It started when I realized that *I am the one who chooses the league in which I want to play*.

If I had decided to be a "nobody" all my life, I would probably have been successful at it. But I wanted to *be* successful and I set my sights on

my goal. I decided what kind of clothes I wanted to wear and what hobbies I liked, and I set out to make it all come true.

What do you want to do? Would you like to sell thousands of dollars' worth of paintings a year in outdoor shows, or do you want to become the next Picasso? It's all up to you. Don't try to

The home of Jerry Caplan, a sculptor and former professor of art, shows that he's given his art a primary place in his life. His living space, accented by his artwork and handmade furniture, is connected to a huge two-story studio with tall doors to accommodate large pieces of sculpture—and the studio opens onto a sculpture garden.

2

hide behind some imagined limitation, such as "that's the only type of thing I can do." You are the one who decides where you will be successful. No one is going to tell you to step to the front of the line . . . everyone is too busy trying to get there themselves. It's easy to play the role of the "misunderstood" artist. Poor you; no one likes your work; no one ever appreciates you. Baloney!

What you have to do is tell the world and yourself that you *are* worth something. It's amazing how people respond to positive thinking. When articles were first written about me, I was astounded at how people believed what was written just because it appeared in print. I had won a number of awards, but nobody took much notice until an article appeared in the *Pittsburgh Post Gazette*. Then even my friends began to believe I was an artist. Didn't they realize I had told the reporter everything he wrote? I could have said anything—but I didn't. It's better to stick to the truth, but record all of your accomplishments in their best light.

The world appreciates those who appreciate themselves. If you don't like what you are and what you are doing, then *change*. You can do it— and it doesn't matter whether you are male or female. Being an artist is not a sex issue. You might run into a problem along the way if, for example, you are a parent or the sole provider for your family. But there are usually ways to deal with such problems. Deserting your brush will probably only compound your difficulties.

Full-Time Art

Creating pictures must be the focal point of an artist's life. One of the most devastating ideas to stick in an artist's mind is that art cannot be pursued on a full-time basis. Nonsense! You don't have to waste your time doing something else to make a living.

Can you imagine a plumber working full time as a sign painter and trying to build up a plumb-ing business on the side? "That's no way to start a business," you'd say. "You have to go at it full time." The same is true for artists.

Of course there's a big demand for plumbers, but there is also one for artists if you look around. Most plumber's work can be done by many a handyman, but there is no handyman or handywoman in the world who can produce a work of art by *you*. Each artist is unique. No one else can produce exactly what another artist can produce.

Plumbers have enough confidence to work at plumbing full time because they are sure of their work demand. Most artists aren't that confident. But artists often bring on a lack of demand by lack of determination in producing and display-ing. If a plumber never went out to work or never let it be known that he did work or refused to give a well thought-out price for his work, do you think he would get much work to do? If you pooh-pooh the idea of comparing your work to a plumber's, ask yourself, "Do I take myself seriously?"

As with any other profession, when you are well prepared, you can make a living at art. Being a successful artist is at least 90 percent hard work and maybe, if you are lucky, 10 percent talent. Once you realize that, you are on your way. Your worst enemy is yourself: Don't limit your horizons.

It takes work, *real* work, to be an artist. There is no time for making a living elsewhere. Some of you work a nine-to-five job. Remember: work-ing at anything that takes you away from art de-feats your goal. I'm hoping that if you do work from nine to five, your job is art-related. In that case, my wrath does not reach you in the same intensity as it would if your job were outside the art field.

If you do have a full-time job, you can still become a successful artist. If you can find five hours a day at least four days a week to work at painting, you can graduate to living by your brush alone. What would happen, though, if you gave yourself a real chance by borrowing enough money to live on for a year? Borrow against your house or your good looks, whatever you've got, and set out to live the way you want to. Are you one of those who stays tied to a unhappy job just because you have built up some retirement or you have hospitalization? Believe it or not, you can get those same things for yourself (see Chapter 10).

You have two duties to yourself.
- To train yourself as well as possible; become as *good* as you can.
- To be true to yourself and be an artist. Work at it, and at *it*, only.

Why Copy Success? Be a Success

Artists talk a lot about influence and pull—politics in the art world. Does it exist? I suppose so, but I contend politics might get you in the spot in the art world where you want to be, but can never keep you *out* when you are good enough. What is "good"? Any artist who sincerely works to create pictures entirely his own is a "good" artist. As far as politics go, the best game to play is one of "kindness."

A successful artist friend of mine reminds me always that there is room for each of us in the world, that there is never any reason to compete with any other artist. If you are truly creating your own art, there is no competition. I've watched many potential artists become so fascinated with what makes others successful, and so busy trying to copy those successes, they forget to put the required effort into their own individuality. As a result, much potential is wasted because the effort is spent in the wrong direction.

In the process of trying to copy others' success, artists often fret about being accepted into professional groups. I hear colleagues bemoaning the fact that they were not accepted into this or that group or show. If such organizations are important for personal prestige, or useful as stepping stones to public recognition, there may be reason to seek membership. But is it important to aspire to any outside "entity" when your real goal is to be an "entity" yourself? There are a lot of associations in the art world. I've helped to start some of them, so I'm not deriding them, but I wonder if Andrew Wyeth or Georgia O'Keeffe ever had nagging worries about being accepted into any such group.

Most of the greats in art history had to start from nowhere, too. Read about them and see just how they went about it. Good reference books are readily available.

And Now to Courage

How do you find the courage to live by your brush alone? Courage is an elusive quality. It is rarely possessed, but it can be acquired. When I first set out on my own, I was terrified. I packed what I thought I needed in my little car, leaving the rest of my belongings in storage. This was a personal choice—I felt the need to travel right then. I began by peddling paintings around the country to make it possible to get where I wanted to go.

It turned out I took things I did not need. Some odd things, however, were necessary. Who needs a ceramic hand-thrown pot over one-and-a-half feet high in a car? I did. That pot had been given to me by the Pittsburgh Watercolor Society after I'd served as president. I needed tokens of esteem and affection right then. They strengthened my courage.

It was a crazy two years before I settled down. Many times I was tempted to quit and work for a regular paycheck, but I stuck to my goal. I told myself the minute I relied on anything but my painting to provide my living, I would be selling myself short. I am what I am—an artist. I live by my brush alone.

4

Jerry Caplan
Professor Emeritus of Art
Chatham College
Pittsburgh, Pennsylvania

Talk about an artist who has the courage to live by his art—Jerry Caplan does. Sculptor and painter as well as teacher, Caplan knows the value of being an artist full time, as well as the difficulties of trying to make ends meet. He has won many awards in both painting and sculpture and has had one-person shows. An innovator in clay, he developed the Pipe Sculpture Workshops taught in Ohio, Pennsylvania, and California using factory facilities.

Q. *Do you think of yourself as a professor of art or an artist?*

A. Hopefully they are one and the same. One always *learns* from teaching. I guess I identify myself as an artist/teacher. If one really enjoys learning, one appreciates the pleasure of helping others do the same and seeing "the light of understanding" in the eyes of the student. Now that I am retiring from formal teaching, I will continue to "help" oth-ers through workshops, lectures, and seminars. The advantage of my living experience makes available a great storehouse from which to draw.

Q. *What was your first job?*

A. My first job of real importance was working for a manikin manufacturer modeling life-size manikins in clay. I had done some freelance commercial art, display work for a department store, photographed parties, painted signs—but my most exciting job was working in a clay factory where they made terra cotta pipe. That job turned my life around. It was there that I developed my philosophy of the cylinder, and the cylinder continues to serve as both the armature and the skin of my sculpture.

Q. *So you've never really worked at anything noncreative?*

A. I've always held the belief that being next to art materials was important. Nowadays there are lots of materials that one finds in the creation of art—paper, cardboard, scrap metal, wood epoxies, glass, etc.—so one doesn't have to think of art materials only in the traditional sense. The artistic spirit will find ways to put these to work in the service of art.

Q. *Did you ever have any times when you didn't know if you could make a living?*

A. Oh sure, when I moved down to North Carolina, early in my career, and opened a school and gallery. There were many times the sale of a painting barely saved the day! The painting went out the door as the landlord came up the steps to collect the rent. But there were other jobs I did to make ends meet. I worked for a painting *contractor* and used my artistic skills to paint straight lines down miles of corridors in a hospital . . . but this led to a mural contract for a bank that the painting contractor was decorating. I had never made a painting by the square yard before. The $1500 that I got for the job went right into a beautiful, shiny, taffy apple red, 1946 wood-body station wagon. Wouldn't that be a treasure now?

Q. *You have made some discoveries. If you were a scientist, you'd be in research?*

A. All of my discoveries have been made in the service of creativity. The scientist deals in facts while the artist deals in imagination. I have discovered that metal can be combined with clay at low temperatures to produce sculpture. I have learned through trial and error that one can make drawings on clay using smoke through a stencil. I have discovered that highly glazed sculpture can be motorized and casts beautiful patterns on the walls and ceiling when struck with a narrow beam spotlight. Discovering that sculpture can be made out of sewer pipe extrusions has led to a whole body of sculpture that couldn't have been done any other way.

Q. *Let's get back to the clay factory. You made sewer pipes, did you not?*

A. No, I counted how many pipes were made every ten minutes. A boring job, so to stay awake, I took some pipes off the line and started carving them with a simple palette knife. This led to more elaborate work and had a profound effect on my total work. While I know the power of the cylinder as a form, I have been able to "tame" it and produce very biomorphic pieces by shaping the cylinder from within as well as from without.

Q. *Sensuality seems to be a recurring theme in your work. Why?*

A. I have always found the female form appealing. While I do other subjects, the female form continues to be a source of inspiration and excitement. It has been a symbol of love and beauty for centuries. After all— women are the vessels of civilization. The female form can be seen as a metaphor for regeneration, wholeness, infinity, and life. Women are the other half of men.

Q. *Togetherness and separation at the same time?*

A. I am concerned with the relationship between man and woman. One needs the other . . . these are two forms that are interdependent but at the same time . . . independent, each having their own identity.

Q. *You do both painting and sculpture. Which is the real you?*

A. While most of my work is in sculpture and ceramics, I do continue to paint. In fact, some of my sculpture is painted! It's like having a canvas wrapped *around* a form. But the main thing is that I continue to think of myself as an artist who is creating. I have always refused to work at anything else.

Q. *What advice would you give a young artist who wanted to be "just like you"?*

A. Everyone ought to be unique. A young artist should find a fresh method of personal expression. The key is to have faith in oneself and regard oneself as a creative force—no matter what the material might be. Be an artist first—use your sensitivity and react to relationships. Remember, you are the "poet" who serves as the receiver and the transmitter of artistic vision.

CHAPTER TWO

Building Your Credentials

In the early stages of your career, it is sometimes hard to figure out how to get started. You don't have any credentials to back you up and you don't really feel professional. The trick is to build your credentials one step at a time—first exhibiting in nonjuried local shows (perhaps outdoor shows or shows in shopping malls) and then moving on to juried shows, small one-person shows, gallery shows, and, hopefully, some day to one-person museum shows.

It's easy to get discouraged in the beginning. The struggle to establish yourself consumes much of your energy and you may not see anything you do as a success. Remember that the mere struggle to set up your booth at a show is an accomplishment (a success, a potential credential), and the first time you do that, or make a sale or get asked to exhibit, you are building your credentials.

You build credentials by working hard to accomplish goals, and then by *recording* the accomplishments. That's all credentials really are—proofs of your accomplishments. This chapter will show you how to get started.

Step One: Define Your Market

Finding your own niche is the first step, because the type of credentials you need is governed by the kind of artist you want to be. If you haven't found your niche yet, Chapters 5 through 8 will help.

In building credentials, look for what will impress your chosen market. If you have decided to make your mark through galleries, don't waste time trying to land an illustration job with a magazine, even if the editor himself suggests it. There will always be well-meaning friends around with suggestions about what you should do. Artists seem particularly susceptible to this kind of flattery. Unless the suggestion fits your own plans, don't be tempted. It's so easy to be led down blind alleys. If a friend says you should illustrate a book (when you are in the middle of an abstract painting series) or suggests you start

making your living by painting cats (just because you produced one good cat sketch), smile sweetly or punch him in the mouth—whichever suits your fancy—but don't listen. Follow your own lead to your own goals.

A certain amount of "dues" have to be paid, however, and they are a different cup of tea from the sidetracking ideas of friends. There are some tedious things you must fit into your plans. Don't try to skip the beginning stages of your career. For instance, if you have chosen fine art as your niche, you may have to spend time sitting in the local, outdoor shows before you move on to the galleries. If you choose to be a commercial artist, you may have to accept assignments you don't like before you can be selective. Keep samples of your jobs; and keep records of sales or awards in outdoor shows.

Step Two: Determine Your Worth

A way of judging your own worth is needed next. How do you know how good you are? Be realistic. Find out what your clientele thinks. Most art directors and gallery directors are willing to talk to you about this. The hard part is listening. Don't take offense. If you want to make money as an artist, you have to please someone, somewhere. But take heart. What one gallery owner hates, another will love. Get several opinions and take what pleases you from all of their ideas. In other words, pick brains.

Get the opinions of the general art-buying public as well. Early in your career in fine art, outdoor shows are a great opportunity to discover a cross section of people's likes and dislikes. People will tell you what they appreciate. Eavesdrop on their comments as they walk past and talk with them directly. They love to talk and you can educate them as they inform you. But be careful. Don't allow yourself to be governed by what the public may want, but don't shut them out. Use only those ideas that fit into your own way of thinking. You will be surprised at what develops. When I choose popular subjects, I treat them my own way. I have won awards with paintings that have come out of a popular series on one subject, such as eagles. When you are immersed in the kind of painting you feel is interesting, when you are being totally creative, people become interested in what you are thinking. They will want *your* work because *you* did it. You touched them and opened a new avenue of thought for them. This is what art is all about.

When your work is selling well, it is time to raise prices. Sometimes, when it isn't selling, it is time to raise prices. People judge what they get by what they pay. Once, when things were slow, I doubled the price of my portraits and sold seven in one week.

Judge your worth by *your* accomplishments. Don't dwell on what you *haven't* done and don't judge your worth by what others think. If you judge your worth by others' opinions, you won't succeed. There are so many types of people in this world that you will always find conflicting opinions. Trying to heed them all is a sure way to constant confusion.

Work for those who like you for yourself. *Everyone* doesn't have to appreciate you; all you require is enough buyers to keep you working as an artist. When you become famous, everyone will *say* they appreciate you, but half of them won't know why.

My main criteria for a good piece of art is that it be truly creative, that it came from my own mind and is not imitative. Design and planning count, but most of all, good painting is not imitative.

Step Three: Build a Personality that Sells

Building a *selling personality* along with your credentials is most important. Let's talk about how this can be accomplished.

It helps in selling your work and acquiring credits to be pleasant. Don't have a chip on your shoulder. Some artists like to feel that the world is being unkind to them. I remember, with distaste, one artist, a young man I met at an outdoor show—one of the places where I "paid my dues." This young watercolorist was an annual exhibitor. The first year I met him, our booths were side by side. I was amazed to observe him turn his back on many potential customers because they'd ask questions he felt were beneath his dignity. Still, he and I had a fairly good rapport. We manned each other's booths at coffee breaks and had some good discussions on art, but I was annoyed at his "antiestablishment" attitude. Art is so flexible and innovative that no one can ever really find the "establishment." Any artist who is worrying about it is fighting a ghost that he need not even conjure. Despite all this, I found the young man interesting and his work pleasing.

Two years went by before I saw him again. When we met this time, he had his hands full of display racks, but no paintings by which I could identify him. We greeted each other warmly. Unfortunately, he looked a lot like a photographer I'd met at the same show two years earlier. I mistakenly asked how his photography was going. He bristled and glared at me and said, "Well, it's clear you don't remember my work, but I remember yours well and I *did* like it." (My work was sitting on the sidewalk right in front of me.) He turned on his heel and walked away, never speaking to me again during that show even though I tried to explain. I had liked his work, too. Should I be condemned because his face looked like someone else's? Nor was I the only victim of such petulant behavior. I saw him do the same thing to customers.

This kind of attitude is one we should fight constantly. Nobody *deserves* respect; one *earns* it. I fight my ego, and boost it at the same time, by helping people remember me. I say something like, "Well, hi! Good to see you again. Remember me? I'm the crazy lady who paints on tissue paper." All this is said before they can be embarrassed if they fail to instantly recall who I am.

Make it a habit to think of others first. This may sound Pollyanna-ish but it works—even when you become a noted artist. How much nicer to be remembered as that famous artist who bothered to worry if someone remembered her, than to be thought of as that egotist who believed he should be remembered just because he thought he was famous. Building a personality that sells you as an artist actually builds your credentials, because the more you sell yourself, the more opportunities for accomplishment you create. So smile, and be pleasant. It pays.

Recording Accomplishments

As soon as you begin to achieve, start keeping a good record of your accomplishments and copies of any publicity connected with your shows and sales. Get a filing cabinet. Keep letters between you and clients plus letters of recommendation. Save the award certificates from shows, records and programs from your one-person shows when they come along, gallery requests—anything that shows the progress of your career. These papers actually are your credentials. Start a *record sheet* listing all of these accomplishments and organize them so that you can use the information profitably. When you are commissioned to do a painting, win any recognition, or make a sale in a show, put that on your record sheet so you won't forget it. Yes, you will forget even important accomplishments as your work grows. Record any job, any small honor, any news clipping about yourself, no matter how small. This sheet is only for you to see and to keep your own record straight. You will use excerpts from it to prepare your finished *résumé*, the written record of your credentials. A résumé is what you hand to potential clients to give them a picture of your experience. Preparing your résumé is discussed in depth in Chapter 4.

To prove the value of well-kept records: One of the first things put on my private record sheet came back to haunt me in a pleasant way and it

"Seated Eagle," Edna Wagner Piersol, 28 x 22 inches, watercolor on tissue paper coated with wax.

Several times eagle paintings like this one have saved my life and kept me eating. Not only did I sell one to a company with "eagle" in its name just by walking in and introducing myself, but I've also traded a few for room and board.

might have been easily forgotten if not recorded. This is how it went. When I was about fourteen years old, I painted a watercolor of a string of perch I had caught. I mixed my paint with water from the lake in which the fish had been caught. The watercolor painting won the top award in the Grange Fair Art Exhibit in the adult competition, which was fabulous to me at that age. Who would think that childish award still useful? It was. Years later, a newspaper writer was doing an article on a show in which I had a watercolor of an abstract fish. I mentioned the earlier award to him and he was immediately interested. He used my story, complete with a photo of me and my painting with the show director looking over my shoulder, as the focus of his article. The whole article was improved because no photo had been scheduled until the appealing "gim-mick" presented itself.

Keep *clippings* on file along with your résumé information. Put everything that is ever printed about you in folders in chronological order. Keep a special cross-reference card file on them with subjects such as "fish" or "blue paintings" or "travel experience." Many of your clippings will be useful in a number of categories.

Keep *color slides* of your paintings, made immediately after finishing each piece. Use these slides to enter shows (see Chapter 6) and for small, informal showings when you are making presentations of your work. Also have black and white glossy photographs, made by a professional, of all your best works. These will be invaluable when you get your presentations together.

Building Sales

How do you find work? Go and look for it. Meet people. Being seen and heard are your biggest assets at the beginning. When you are seen, your work will also be seen. It is emotionally hard for artists to seek exposure of their work because producing art is so personal. We can't help feeling that a rejection of our work is a rejection of ourselves. Fight this attitude. Try to look at your sales approach as though you were selling apples instead of pictures. If you knock on someone's door and ask if they want to buy apples, they might tell you they want oranges, or they might say they had just bought apples. You wouldn't have a nervous breakdown over that, would you?

Try to make the selling fun. That way it won't be so hard on you. Learn to look at a potential buyer as someone you want to meet and enjoy rather than someone to be conquered. Try to fill the buyer's needs. Reach out.

Knock on doors. One day I was traveling through Georgia and I needed money. It was in the period of my life when I was searching to find myself after a divorce. Traveling on my own I was

I HAVE FALLEN IN LOVE WITH AND WILL SOON BE STARTING A SERIES OF PAINTINGS OF

OCEAN AVENUE

I would like to include your home in this series. I already have an order from Jim Plum. Please phone me at your convenience to let me tell you about the Ocean Ave. Series.

At this point you can have some input as to the style of the work, size, price, etc.
BUT — CALLING TO DISCUSS THE SERIES PUTS YOU UNDER NO OBLIGATION TO BUY A PAINTING OF YOUR HOME

Artist: EDNA WAGNER PIERSOL
Address Here, Happiness FL 32541
(000) 037- 0080

This is the type of brochure I use when seeking painting commissions of homes. It not only introduces me to the homeowners, but also gives them a hint of how charming their homes could look as paintings. I make it easy for customers to call to find out more by including my phone number.

literally peddling paintings out of the back of my car. I had an appointment at an Atlanta office building. When I arrived, the office had a note on the door telling me the owner had to go out for half an hour and to please wait. Next door was an insurance agency with the word "Eagle" in its name. There was an eagle painting in my portfolio. I was in a good mood that day, although on the verge of starving. Maybe hunger had made me lightheaded, but it also gave me extra courage. Two pleasant young men were visible through the window and the office walls were bare.

I walked in and introduced myself, naming some of my credits in my introduction. I think I said something about being the artist lady who sold from the back of her car, that my most famous painting was of an eagle, and that it was in a museum collection. I told them their agency name demanded an eagle on the wall and that I had one in my car. The situation was bizarre enough to be fun for all and could be taken lightly, yet seriously at the same time. I was careful not to be too pushy, but before long they were asking to see the eagle. When I left, they had a new painting on their wall and I had enough money to travel on to Pennsylvania. I ate well that week and added a new credit to my name.

Another time, when I needed some new commissions, I was struck by a brainstorm while sightseeing. I got out my sketch pad and went to work. I sketched one or two houses, then I took photos. I went back to my studio and painted a small watercolor that would reproduce easily. I had it reduced to a size that would fit on a nice little brochure and wrote a neat letter to be printed with it, informing homeowners that I was beginning a series of watercolors of each of their houses. I added my address and phone number, and waited. When commissions resulted, my credentials had grown.

"Looking for work" can be done in local art exhibits. You'll find art show listings in art magazines. Watch your local newspaper to find shows being held in your area. Often there are shows open to any artist. Enter your work exactly as described in the printed information that is always given out about an exhibit. Be careful to follow the directions to the letter. See Chapters 5 and 6 for more information on entering shows.

When the show is on the wall, be present and available. Meet everyone you can. If you are shy, make yourself talk to everyone who shows any interest in your work. They will be interested in you if you show an interest in them. I've even walked up to people looking at my paintings and said to them, "I wouldn't give you two cents for a Piersol painting." As they turn to me, their expressions are extremely interesting. By that time I'm laughing and introducing myself and we become friends. I don't know what I'll do the day someone says to me, "Neither would I." Oh well, take the bitter with the better. If you keep forcing yourself to meet people, someone will want more artwork and you'll be there at the right time.

Creating Your Own Publicity

Another way to find work with your brush early in your career is to be open to doing some charity work for the publicity it offers. *Getting publicity in order to find work is a big goal when you begin to live solely by your art.* Artists are notorious for being impractical. Sometimes we don't realize that we can be "super-talented" and still be undiscovered. It is important for artists to sell themselves. If the first order of business is to become a good artist, then the second is to start to publicize yourself. Build your credentials, then see that they pay off.

Good public relations will not make up for weak art, but good art without good PR will go nowhere. Promotion, or "image," is invaluable and cannot be replaced. Don't kid yourself and think artists become well known because of "merit." Success almost never depends on merit alone.

When "seeking publicity" be sure it is handled subtly. Don't be pushy or obvious. People should not realize that publicity is what you're after. Try to find ways to make yourself interesting and newsworthy. Here is where your record sheet does its work. Go over it regularly and see

Description of Available Workshops:

These are One-Day Workshops, 9:30 a.m. to 2:30 p.m. (longer time possible if requested.) Each workshop is a self-contained one-day study. Any combination of workshops can be scheduled to arrange a 2 to 5 day watercolor clinic. Two-day weekend sessions are very popular.

Facing the WHITE PAPER
Featuring the one-stroke watercolor

White paper . . . the great equalizer! Watercolorists have all fought it at one time or another. It requires attack. Edna Piersol has developed a way of attacking with one stroke that establishes the whole painting in one swoop of the brush. Beginning students are astounded and students at other levels learn much from this new approach.

In this workshop the teacher also covers the various other approaches to painting a watercolor. Simple exercises that teach the aforementioned will be given. Exercises designed to get the class in the mood to paint. Students will be told what pigments to use and how to apply them. They will be given certain things to complete in certain time periods . . . 4 or 5 minutes and sometimes as short as 30 seconds. Ms. Piersol finds that students make tremendous strides in learning by this method. But beginners, you need not be

One-Stroke Watercolor
Collection of the Artist

frightened. It's fun! The exercises will cause the student to learn about composing paintings; application of pigment; color; use of tools; kinds of paper; understanding abstract ideas . . . all without realizing it "'til the light dawns."

This workshop is for beginners to advanced. The instructor has developed a way of teaching that makes each student feel at ease and each learns at his own level.

Facing the COLOR in Watercolor

This one-day workshop is a take off on a seminar that Edna Piersol has been teaching at various colleges. Class will begin with exercises which teach color as it applies to watercolor and get you in the mood to paint. The approach will be the same as in "FACING THE WHITE PAPER," giving the student definite things to do in definite time periods, but the emphasis will be on COLOR which IS the most important ingredient in watercolor. Students will learn about the various properties of pigments; their degree of permanence and transparency, etc.; what warm and cool colors do. Exercises will be given to help the student understand application of color. Paper influence on color will be discussed. This is a self contained study and may be scheduled without any of the other workshops but it is a good follow up to "FACING THE WHITE PAPER."

Ghost of Freedom
Collection of the Artist

Facing the HUMAN FIGURE with Watercolor

The same approach of giving time limits to do certain definitely described exercises. Students absorb a great deal this way. A model will be used, usually clothed unless otherwise requested. As in the other workshops the student will be told what pigments to use and how to apply them.

Facing the OUTDOORS with Watercolor

Once again, the same approach as the other workshops — with time periods to accomplish definite things. This workshop requires a little more planning than the others because a good location is needed. The student will be provided with a very structured workshop, giving one good plan of attack on the out-of-doors.

Facing Making a LIVING . . . as an Artist

All the expertise this artist has mustered in her more than 15 years experience in painting, exhibiting, teaching and advertising work will be placed at the disposal of her students in this workshop. Mrs. Piersol believes firmly that it is not all that hard to make $25,000 to $50,000 per year and even more. Your opportunity is limited only to your desire to work. A certain amount of effort DOES produce a certain amount of money.

Painted with a Credit Card
Collection of Mr. & Mrs. Paul Fitting

what might best be exploited.

Clubs and church groups are always looking for ways to make money. Give them a free lecture demonstration which they can open to the public and get newspaper coverage. When you do a lecture or demonstration, you might get a commission from someone. If you aren't a public speaker, arrange a painting raffle. To live by your brush alone, a lot of time must be spent doing things that do not pay off immediately. Look for ways of getting around this fact of life. Try getting a club member to purchase a painting at a nominal fee to cover your expenses. Get as realistic a price as you can. Perhaps your benefactor will pay close to your original asking price. She can then give the painting to the club to raffle off. This allows the buyer to deduct the painting from her taxes, the club to make money, and you to have your expenses paid.

There will be other times when it may enhance your reputation to give the painting outright. But watch this procedure—it may start a snowball rolling that you don't want. Your object, always, is to make your work pay your living expenses. Don't lose sight of that goal. It is a goal different from the one of being a good artist. They are two separate categories. If you have not convinced a club member, or the club itself, to purchase a painting in advance, try another approach. Be persistent in your trials to sell. Go one step *beyond* your feelings of propriety. This is hard to do, and worse if you're a little shy. I've found one pleasant way to be persistent is to single out someone in whom you have sensed a spark of interest, and simply tell that person, in private, that you would really like one of your paintings to go into his collection. Potential buyers find such an approach hard to resist. I always

My workshop brochure goes to clubs and other organizations that might be interested in sponsoring one of my workshops. This side explains how the workshops are structured and what topics can be covered. The reverse side lists my credentials and leaves room for a mailing label.

Writing a Press Release

Here are some tips on writing press releases from Keets Rivers, former columnist of Sunshine Artists U.S.A., whose work and views on art shows you will see on pages 59-60.

At the top of your first page, *center* the words *Press Release*. Always place the contact person's name, address, and phone number in the upper right-hand side of the first page or center it. Skip two spaces and write your release date and underline it. For a lengthy release, skip a double space, then give—

1. WHAT
2. WHERE
3. WHEN
4. WHY (if needed)

Then give more detailed information, starting with a very clear opening sentence that has the same information as the What, Where, When from above. Often it may be the *only* thing you get in the paper, so make it clear and concise. Your press release must be typed and double-spaced, and it's best to keep it to one page—never more than two. Anything longer, as a rule, goes in the waste basket.

After the Who, What, Where, When, Why of a press release, a *"shout"* sentence that will perk up interest is a good idea. Sometimes this sentence will be picked up and used in the press release. Another important sentence is the last, or closing, sentence. Be sure to mention facts such as how long the work will be on display or the closing date of the show.

End your press release with—30—(preferred) or * * *, centered on the line.

Submit your release at least one week in advance for a daily paper and two weeks in advance for a weekly paper. If there is a certain day of the week art news is featured in your paper, you may

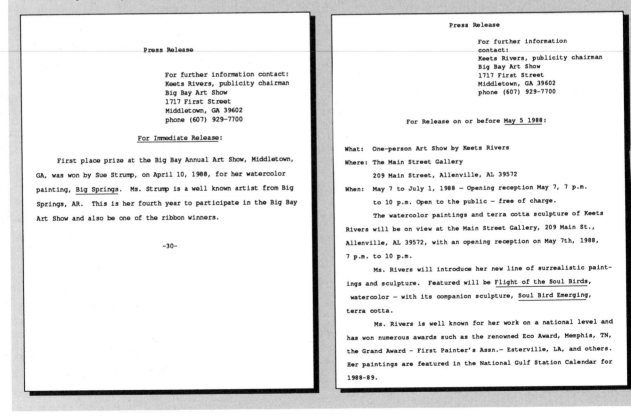

```
                    Press Release

                    For further information contact:
                    Keets Rivers, publicity chairman
                    Big Bay Art Show
                    1717 First Street
                    Middletown, GA 39602
                    phone (607) 929-7700

          For Immediate Release:

     First place prize at the Big Bay Annual Art Show, Middletown,
GA, was won by Sue Strump, on April 10, 1988, for her watercolor
painting, Big Springs. Ms. Strump is a well known artist from Big
Springs, AR. This is her fourth year to participate in the Big Bay
Art Show and also be one of the ribbon winners.

                         -30-
```

```
                    Press Release

                    For further information
                    contact:
                    Keets Rivers, publicity chairman
                    Big Bay Art Show
                    1717 First Street
                    Middletown, GA 39602
                    phone (607) 929-7700

          For Release on or before May 5 1988:

What:  One-person Art Show by Keets Rivers
Where: The Main Street Gallery
       209 Main Street, Allenville, AL 39572
When:  May 7 to July 1, 1988 — Opening reception May 7, 7 p.m.
       to 10 p.m. Open to the public — free of charge.
       The watercolor paintings and terra cotta sculpture of Keets
Rivers will be on view at the Main Street Gallery, 209 Main St.,
Allenville, AL 39572, with an opening reception on May 7th, 1988,
7 p.m. to 10 p.m.
       Ms. Rivers will introduce her new line of surrealistic paint-
ings and sculpture. Featured will be Flight of the Soul Birds,
watercolor — with its companion sculpture, Soul Bird Emerging,
terra cotta.
       Ms. Rivers is well known for her work on a national level and
has won numerous awards such as the renowned Eco Award, Memphis, TN,
the Grand Award - First Painter's Assn.— Esterville, LA, and others.
Her paintings are featured in the National Gulf Station Calendar for
1988-89.
```

want to use that day for your *release date* ("*to be released on May 4, 1988*"). If you wish you may also send black-and-white photos with your release. They may use them; however, large papers often like to send their own photographers, so allow extra time if you are trying for a photo in the paper (which is hard to get, as a rule). The black-and-white photos should be 5 x 7 inches. Do not expect to have any of this returned to you. If they use your photos in the paper you will be lucky. You will even be lucky if they use that one sentence. After all—it was free.

Here are examples of three different types of press releases. The first is a very brief announcement that could be printed at any time. The second is slightly longer, so it gives a quick summary of the important details first. It also gives a release date. The third is a public service announcement to be read on radio or television, so it needs a little different handling.

```
                              Press Release

                         For further information
Public Service           contact:
release for TV           Keets Rivers, publicity chairman
or radio                 Big Bay Art Show
                         1717 First Street
                         Middletown, GA 39602
                         phone (607) 929-7700


                        For immediate release


time 15 seconds                                     51 words

     Watercolor artist Keets Rivers will give a watercolor demonstra-
tion at the Midtown Public Library, 729 First St., N.W., Big Springs,
AR, on June 10, 1988 at 7 p.m.  The demonstration given by Ms. Rivers
is sponsored by the Big Springs Art Assn.  The demonstration is free
and open to the public.

                             - 30 -
```

follow up any kind of interest with one phone call. I'm never obtrusive, just interested in having a new collector involved in my work and owning it.

Promotional Pieces

Aim for one good publicity accomplishment per month. You can do your own publicity when none other is available, or until you build up enough confidence to try for splashy things like news articles. Remember my Ocean Avenue series? In Chapter 4, I give more directions on preparing promotional pieces, because to increase your publicity, you will need to have some kind of general mailing and handout pieces to give to prospective buyers. Get good help on this and pay for it.

I have a brochure on my workshops that was laid out by a designer who traded his work for one of my paintings. The brochure contains good black-and-white photos of five of my most accepted paintings, a photo of me, and a description of the five kinds of workshops I present to art groups. I have another card with a good reproduction of one of my most appealing portraits. I hand these out to two very different kinds of clients: the portrait cards to people interested in fine art portraits and the workshop brochures to prospective students. I also mail these out, and that is what I am suggesting to you.

I do a lot of speaking to clubs and organizations. Giving a free lecture at a club meeting usually produces several portrait and painting commissions. Giving a lecture to an art group usually produces a workshop or two. Clubs usually get their programs for the following year set up months ahead of time. I've found that a mailing around the middle of January (when people are just pulling out of the post-holiday doldrums) gets the most attention.

I send a pretty promotion piece like my portrait card or my workshop brochure (depending on the kind of club) with a cover letter. It is good to do some research about the club and have an

A PORTRAIT

by
EDNA WAGNER PIERSOL

mailing address:
303 Primrose Circle
Destin, FL 32541

to see more of this artist's work
call for an appointment

(904) 837-3380

This card lets people know I accept portrait commissions. It shows one of my portraits and gives the vital information. A brief statement giving my philosophy of portrait painting is printed on the back.

"angle" as I have in the sample letter, but sometimes I do a "cold" mailing just like a "cold" call. One of those letters is also shown.

Other good mailing months for promotion pieces are September and October—to seek commissions from clients thinking ahead to Christmas. Just a painting reproduction card with the handwritten words, "Come see my work," or "Call for an appointment to visit my studio" will do the trick here.

You may become so busy that you have to create a waiting list for next Christmas, but mail when you get *their* attention, not for your convenience.

If you are a commercial artist, you *must* keep your name constantly before art directors without being too obtrusive. A neat card sent to art directors you already know, with a reproduction of your work and a note on the back, accomplishes this. Handwritten notes, even quickies on the margins of printed pieces, do wonders. The personal touch is the icing on the cake. It makes the receiver, no matter how important, feel *more* important.

Building your credentials is your most important "early career" or "starting over" task. So start by working hard; then keep a complete record of your accomplishments. You never know what will pay off. Get the record out before the public. Be ready when opportunity knocks to give information about yourself. It's hard to be egotistical, but try it—you might like it. Brag a little, but do it gently. Nobody loves a bore. Try my three A's for *accreditation*: accomplish—account—assert. First: Accomplish the work. Second: Keep a detailed account of what you have done. Last, but by no means least: Assert that you have done some great work.

Moving On

Be sure you don't confine yourself to the beginning stage of your career after it's time to move on. This is a mistake 90 percent of all struggling

Sea Catch Studio
Artist: Edna Wagner Piersol

33 Address Ave, Town FL 01020
(000) 807-0080

Jan. 6, 1989

Jane Friendly, President
Prospect Woman's Club
Lovely Lane
Prospect, FL 01020

Dear Mrs. Friendly:

Enclosed is my portrait card. I want to offer the Prospect Woman's Club a
free lecture during the fall season, 1989.

One of your members, Mrs. Allgood, recently mentioned to me that your
project for this year is helping gifted children. One of the lectures in
my repertoire is titled "The Creative Child" and is based on reminiscences
of my own childhood and how my mother and father and grandparents dealt
with this strange little "artist being" who had landed among them. I will
also exhibit 4 or 5 of my paintings or bring slides, if you wish, and I'll
be glad to answer questions on commissions and art classes for children.

Although I believe you know of me, the following is an excerpt from my
resume to let you know what I have to offer.

ARTIST, AUTHOR/LECTURER, CONSULTANT, WORKSHOP INSTRUCTOR: author of _Living
by Your Brush Alone_; listed in the World Who's Who of Women; member of the
National League of American Pen Women in both Arts and Letters, founder of
the Pittsburgh Aquarelle Watercolor Exhibit; a founder of the Kentucky Watercolor Society; Charter Member of the Southern Watercolor Society; former Art Director of _Beaux Arts Magazine_, Louisville, KY; active in portrait and other commission painting, art societies, and in professional
exhibiting.

REPRESENTED BY:
Pittsburgh Center for the Arts, 5th and Shady, Pittsburgh, PA
Sea Catch Studio, Destin, FL 32541

Please phone me at the above number if your club is interested. Thank
you.

Sincerely,

Edna Wagner Piersol

This cover letter shows how important it is to do some research on any group you contact. By talking to a club member, I found a perfect angle for approaching the group that
fit in with their interests and yet allowed me to introduce my
work to them.

Sea Catch Studio
Artist: Edna Wagner Piersol

33 Address Ave, Town FL 01020
(000) 807-0080

Jan. 6, 1989

Hello,

This is to announce that I will be available for lectures and demonstrations for the spring and fall season 1989.

Please contact me for more information on painting demonstrations or
on lectures titled:

"The Creative Child."
"Anyone Can Learn to Paint."
"Would Your Child Make a Good Portrait?"

Fee: $150 plus expenses. Free lectures are sometimes arranged for
worthy causes and non-profit groups.

Enclosed is my portrait card and an excerpt from my resume.

Sincerely,

Artist's Name

Sometimes a "cold" cover letter—one sent to someone you
don't know and can't research—can be effective. It's best
to keep these short and simple.

artists make because they are afraid to move on. When you begin to feel confident in one arena, move up the ladder to whatever is next, in your judgment. If you feel it is time to enter juried shows, find a local or regional show you feel comfortable with and enter it. If you think it's time to exhibit in galleries, begin to look for one. If it's time to raise prices, do it.

Claire Justine, from Shelbyville, Kentucky, is a good example of an artist who knows the value of moving ahead. At one time she was a watercolor artist who taught lessons, judged exhibits, and painted—she was busy and productive but wasn't getting her art in front of the public.

Since she had been painting watercolor cards for family and friends, she decided to develop this into a profitable sideline. She contacted the owner of a small card shop in the building where she had a studio, who was delighted to carry her hand-painted cards. Very Personal Greetings was born and quickly expanded to other shops.

Once the card business got going, she began to do small watercolor florals painted on silk, matted and mounted in narrow gold or silver frames, which she marketed to small gift and museum shops. Later, after she moved to Texas and reestablished her business there, she also opened her own gallery in an indoor market featuring arts and crafts, where she carried her major paintings as well as the cards, silk paintings, and posters.

Eventually she gave up greeting cards in favor of painting and marketing small watercolors to hotels and hospital gift shops. She's also branched out into collage, pastels, printmaking, papermaking—"and even the design of needlepoint canvas for customers who have bought my paintings and wanted a companion piece."

This kind of expansion and growth is essential for an artist, particularly one who wants to be a full-time artist. Don't hold yourself back because you lack confidence.

"Golden Moments," Claire Justine, 15 x 20 inches, collage.

CHAPTER THREE

Strategy and Discipline

Exactly how much money do you need to make a living? How will you get it? These are questions to ask when making a plan of attack for living by your brush alone. To answer them, first you'll need to ask yourself more questions. Such as:

How many paintings, sold at your highest price, would produce your living expenses? How many would it take at your lowest price? Do you have enough markets to produce that income? How can you go about getting the markets you need? Where have the bulk of your sales been made? How can you exploit that market even more? Expand to other cities? Advertise more? Make personal contacts?

Sound too tough? Let's look at an example. Say you want to make $20,000 per year. If your paintings are selling for $150, that means you have to produce 133.33 paintings per year to produce $20,000. Let's make it easier on ourselves and say you will produce 135 paintings per year. But you haven't allowed any money for expenses yet. I find that about one-third of the selling price of the paintings drains off in expenses, so that means you will have to produce an extra forty-five paintings to cover expenses. This brings the total to 180 paintings a year. Don't panic. That is one painting every 2.2 days. If you are like me, when you are really rolling, you can start three to five paintings in a day. Painting that much forces you to grow as an artist.

Don't forget, we are selling your paintings at a very low price. You may have to do that for a while. Your price will soon go up. (For more on pricing strategies, see Chapter 10.) When you reach the $2,000 per painting level, you will have to produce less than 1.3 paintings per month to make ends meet. You say you are not ready for $2,000 painting sales yet? Let's try our breakdown with $350 paintings. That only requires you to produce a painting every 4.05 days. Not bad at all. Not even two a week—and your price *will* go up. I found that one portrait per month and one other commission kept me in the income bracket in which I chose to live. There are a lot of advantages that keep an artist in a living style above income level. Let's go on with our plan of attack and see how it all works out.

It's hard for an artist to think in terms of producing half a painting a day or producing one painting every other day. It is much better to carve out large blocks of work. For instance, schedule a show of sixty paintings. That's one-third of your year's work at the low $150-per-painting rate. Work toward that end and plan how you are going to sell those paintings.

Self-Discipline

There are two categories into which your work falls. First comes production. Then comes selling. It would be nice to neatly tie up each group and deal with it separately, but that doesn't work. You must deal with these categories simultaneously.

You must be disciplined in both production and selling. Self-discipline is the key to success. Work a certain number of hours and the same number of hours each day. Don't say you aren't always inspired. Any artist who waits to be inspired is likely to be a starving artist. I'm inspired to eat three times a day, so my brush has to be inspired to move at least three times a day. The best inspiration is picking up the brush. When you feel you do not have an idea in your head, let your technical knowledge take over. You'll find you produce a better painting when your mind is not racing ahead of the brush, tripping over itself and getting your hands all tangled up in the mess.

Organizing Work Hours

You must first set up work hours for yourself—a minimum of five hours a day. Sometimes it does not seem that you are working when you are. I spend a lot of hours each week thinking, writing notes, making blind squiggles (fascinating small designs done with my eyes closed, described later), and humming to myself. A writer friend of mine observed that I worked about two full days per week in order to keep my larder full. But he didn't count all the humming and scribbling, so he misjudged me terribly.

You can't be painting every minute that you are working. A lot of time must be spent doing things, from humming and scribbling to matting, framing, delivering to framers, picking up supplies, writing publicity releases, and keeping records. You don't hold a brush nearly as much as you'd like. But it all must be done. Some days you will paint many more hours than others. I didn't say you can't work eight or ten hours per day or even more; just that you must clear five hours for work each day or you won't succeed.

I know a young woman who gets up at five and has two full hours of painting in before anyone else gets up. She takes a nap with her baby in the afternoon, then puts in another three hours from seven to ten while her husband babysits. Another friend of mine, now one of the most famous watercolor artists in the country, owned a commercial studio. He always put in a full day there only to come home and work four or five hours, four nights per week. Eventually he sold his studio and "retired" to full-time painting and teaching. It's just a matter of organizing. Face that, get at it, and don't be discouraged until you get the hang of it.

Weekly Schedules

Spend time whipping yourself into shape. Develop and write down a schedule. Stick to it religiously. If it does not work, revise it. Revise it *only* if it really doesn't work, not because of laziness or discouragement. There is something that I fight which may be your enemy, too: procrastination. It seems I'll do anything in the world to put off painting, the one thing I love most. I think that no matter how much we love that brush, we also hate it. It forces us to prove ourselves each time we pick it up. When it is time to start to paint, I can always think of ten letters that need answering, two phone calls that must be made— I really must go out to get some masking tape. Procrastination is one more reason that it is imperative to stick to your schedule.

Often it is easier to plan by the week rather than trying to set up a rigid daily schedule. I use about fifteen hours per week in pure painting and sketching. The rest of my work time is scheduled around the painting like this:

Monday	*Morning:* Answer mail. Paint.
	Afternoon: Mount or frame paintings.
Tuesday	*Early Morning:* Paint.
	Late Morning: Keep business appointments, if necessary.
	Afternoon: Appointments or painting.
Wednesday	*Morning:* Paint.
	Afternoon: Do errands, pick up supplies, take work to printers, deliver paintings, etc.
Thursday	*Morning:* Answer mail. Appointments or mounting and framing paintings.
	Afternoon: Appointments or record keeping.
	Evening: Teach painting class.
Friday	Paint all day.
Saturday	Sketching trips; art group activity.
Sunday	Enjoy life a lot. Spend some time in the evening organizing the next week's work.

These hours must be juggled at times to make allowances for appointments at other people's convenience. When this happens, keep a record of how many painting hours you have sacrificed. Make those hours up within the week. Two mornings a week, from eight to nine, I answer letters. Many days I work overtime but never "undertime." Some business calls can be made in the evenings; some evenings I mount or frame paintings, etc.

Tuesday, Wednesday, and Thursday are the best days to schedule the kind of work where interaction with business people is required. Any salesperson will tell you that those days are *the* selling days.

Don't ever forget this is your *job* and it requires the same dedication as any other kind of job. We artists work for ourselves, and the boss — me — is a stickler for getting things accomplished. I've got to tell you, though, my boss rewards me generously. No other boss in this world would give me *all* the profit.

I can't stress enough the need for establishing a work schedule and sticking to it. When you first go into the studio on schedule, you may experience panic. "I have to work, I have to work, I *have* to work *now*?" may be your reaction. Relax. Spend the first hour or so humming and scribbling. Your ideas will fall into place. See what productive work humming can be!

Scheduled Solitude

Being alone and undistracted during the most creative periods of your work week is essential. You must find ways to impress your family and friends with this unalterable fact. That's hard to do. Writers have the same problem. We work at home so people think we don't work at all. Sometimes we even have trouble convincing *ourselves* that our time is not our own. We artists tend to be dreamers and discipline comes hard.

I think it is important to control the kind of people you let into your life. You don't need kibitzers who are time wasters. You must be hardhearted. People always want to know what an artist is doing. They think that because you work at home, you can be bothered at any time. Your retired friends and relatives may take to dropping by your studio for coffee. It will happen without you realizing it.

There have been times in my life when I didn't seem to be getting anything done and I didn't know why. Then I took a good look over the past week. One friend had wanted me to go to a museum with her and explain the latest show; another had wanted to take me shopping to select linens for her niece's wedding gift because I "knew color." If I had worked at a nine-to-five job as a decorator, she would never have presumed to ask; but worse, I, like a fool, had gone.

I love my friends. The hardest thing in the world is to say, "No, I'm sorry, I do not have time." Your friends can make or break your mood. That's why isolating your working time and your working space can't be stressed enough. You are often your own worst enemy on this score, so take time at least once a month to evaluate your work hours and the kind of people you associate with. Try to get the greatest number of people who will inspire you into your life, and those who don't inspire you, *out*. Hardhearted? Yes.

If you do not live alone, schedule your work time when no one else is at home. While I was raising my family, my production hours were nine to three. Sometimes, on days when I was painting, I didn't even eat lunch. My children were in school and that was my only time to work and work hard I did.

If you do not have a time when everyone else leaves the house, consider studio space away from the home or away from its center. You must remove yourself from all distractions. If someone so much as kindly offers you a cup of tea, it may shatter the mood. Some creative stress is good for you and it comes along even in the most secluded situation. Squirrels chatter. Boats pass on the river; a truck rumbles along the road. Just remove all the unwanted interruptions you can. For instance, the telephone: what a jarring shock in the middle of a brushstroke! You can control that evil ring with an answering machine. You can't work without one. My schedule calls for me to turn on the answering machine at nine and not check my calls until ten-thirty or eleven when I feel like a break. Then, if I absolutely have to return a call before noon, I do. Otherwise I check my messages again at four and return all calls

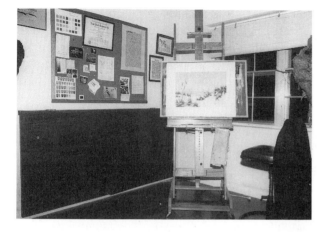

Keets Rivers of Pensacola, Florida, makes the most of her home studio space with a huge worktable made from a door. When not in use, it folds up against the wall.

then. By that time I am so satisfied with getting so much work done that my assurance is sure to show in my voice. So if I go out sketching, or to dinner, or away for several days, I won't miss any commission calls. Sometimes opportunity rings only once. The answering machine is a must, and remembering to turn it on is also essential.

Home Studio Space

I can't say often enough that you have got to take yourself seriously as an artist before anyone else will. One of the musts is good work space—a studio, in other words. Don't even think of working in the garage on your workshop table and moving everything including the smelly house paint when you want to use the saw or working on your kitchen table while your one-year-old smears apricots on the paintings. Those may seem like wonderful solutions to space problems but they will lead to serious misunderstandings with yourself, your clients, and your family.

That doesn't mean you have to have a *lot* of space. Keets Rivers, an artist who lives and works in Pensacola, Florida, has a private studio room in her home that's used for nothing else but her art. It's just 16 x 20 feet, but is all any artist could ask for. She has a huge worktable, made from a door, that's mounted on hinges—when she's not using it, it folds down against the wall and gives her space to set up her easel. The other end of the room contains a no-nonsense office space.

(By the way, when you're setting up your studio space, don't forget the special touches. Rivers' studio has specially balanced lighting, so she can paint at night; a television that lets her keep up with the world; a mirror she uses to check her finished paintings for composition, etc.; a private spot where she can put her feet up and contemplate her latest works in complete peace; a stereo system, since she draws inspiration from music; and a small gallery of ribbons she's won. Those personal touches are important!)

My arrangement for living and working when

Photos by Becky Burnett

23

I had limited space was to combine everything into one apartment. I hid my studio equipment in the kitchen. During nonworking hours, my worktable was covered with a floor-length cloth and looked like a comfortable, slightly oversized kitchen table. When the cloth was removed, a large cube on casters was revealed. One side of the cube was open, exposing shelves. Those shelves held 30 x 40-inch illustration boards, paper, and other gear under the table's ample top.

My other painting paraphernalia, like paint tubes and brushes, was stashed in a fishing kit and stored in the pantry. Over the years, this kit has been my constant companion. It holds everything and follows me all over the country in my car and has even ridden on horseback. It is my studio in a box.

I'm not one for being encumbered with a lot of possessions. I've never envied the artists with huge studios and gigantic equipment. If that's what you like, though, it can't hurt. I do like north light and even when I lived in an apartment I almost always had light streaming in from north-northwest through the balcony window. The light had to travel through my dining room before reaching the kitchen, so I sometimes moved my work into the dining area. The kitchen/studio wasn't overly large, so some other equipment was stored and used in a bedroom. There I had a huge walk-in closet where my photo equipment was stored; a slide projector sat in a table-bin on wheels. The table-bin came from a discount store and had two lower shelf-bins that held slide trays, etc. I pulled it out to use the projector on the white wall and wheeled it to the kitchen when needed. (All my walls were a soft white so they took projection and paintings equally well.) My file cabinet, large painting portfolios, an easel or two, and all other equipment needed for presentations to my clients were also stored in a big closet.

My gallery space was an L-shaped section of my living room. All furniture and visual distrac-

This worktable, which is on wheels and has plenty of room for storage, can be disguised as a dining table.

tions were removed from that area. The walls held about nine paintings at a time and others rested on easels. So, for the price of an apartment, I had studio, gallery, and living space. Of course, I couldn't have an outdoor sign, but my clients were drawn to me by other means of advertising and display described in Chapter 4. I had no trouble from neighbors about clients viewing my work and sitting for portraits. (Check the laws in your area regarding restrictions to operating a business in your home.)

I no longer live in an apartment. When an artist's ability improves, so does his or her life-

Photo by Jean Kirsch

Autry Dye transformed a two-car garage into a studio and gallery, allowing her all the benefits of working at home without sacrificing any living space.

style. A couple of years ago, I decided that I wanted to live near the sea so I set out to do so. I found an inexpensive area in the Florida Panhandle and set up shop. My work sold well there and during that period I opened my own one-artist gallery. But I knew I would also have to keep market areas open in larger cities, so I made arrangements for shipping my work back to art centers in the Northeast. Once I had made a commitment to the sea, other surprising things happened. One of them was meeting a sea captain, who became my husband. I had already learned to "make my life happen," but he is even

better at handling life than I. Between us we have managed to arrange our lifestyle so that we are doing what we most want in life most of the time and I now have a nice studio that overlooks Choctawhatchee Bay and the models for my pelican paintings come right up to my own pilings.

If you have a family, you can still arrange your home to work for you. I have an artist friend who has a gorgeous house in a lovely residential section. Her family has given over to gallery/studio space what would usually be the living room. Their large family room in the back of the house has become the living/family room. The front door leads directly into the studio. When her family leaves in the morning, my friend becomes the total artist. If she has an appointment in the evening, her family is in another world from the studio.

Autry Dye has an even better set-up. She has a full-fledged gallery tucked into her home work space without taking any room from her family. She has found space in a way that most of us would never have thought of. I told you not to even consider working on your garage workshop table, but no one could ever tell Autry not to work in the garage, especially since she and her husband, David, completely revamped it in a unique way. (See the interview at right.)

It's important to let the fact that you are an artist dominate your lifestyle. If you keep your studio back in a spare bedroom, it will be relegated to that status in your life. Your family will treat it as secondary to the rest of living. You will, too. What kind of impression do you make when you take a client to a bedroom to view paintings that you have to pull out from under the bed? When you are living by your brush alone, your style can't be "back bedroom."

Creative Ideas at Work

Getting ideas for work and deciding what you will work on becomes your next project. When you have an idea, go with it. Give it a good hard try. Don't fall into the trap of thinking that anyone can do what you are doing. Our creative minds are so high powered, we forget that others' brains don't work as ours do. Even other creative brains seldom run along the same channel. Never stop doing something because you think that others could do it as well. I have instigated projects that I felt sure everyone else would know how to do. I thought I'd never get recognition for them. To my great delight, I was wrong. I did receive recognition and profit.

If an idea does begin to fail, get out fast! Reinvest your energy in another project right away and don't waste time crying over "spilt paint." It is good to have several painting projects going at one time, so that while one is incubating and another is beginning to fail, still another can be bubbling and keeping your spirits up.

Keep a running record of ideas that will produce income. Have a little notebook that you can keep with you. Write ideas in it for painting subjects and for promotions. A tape recorder is a good friend, too. Keep one with you and talk to yourself anytime. Good ideas are something you don't want to lose.

How long does it take to "drum up" business in an area? I find things begin to happen and money starts to come in after I have been working in an area for about a month. (The kinds of things you have to do to make this happen are covered in Chapters 2 and 4.) It takes time for your name to sink into buyers' minds. If you want to move to a new geographical area, don't be afraid to do it. What works in one area will work in another, but I recommend that you stay near a large urban area—stay accessible. The more people with available money, the more business for you. Look up the average income in an area or check at the area's chamber of commerce before you move. When I was getting established I lived in an area that had a *median* income about 60 percent above that of the rest of the country. If you yearn to move to a mountain top, take into consideration how you will get to a market. If you can get to enough clients from your mountain, go to it. Otherwise, take the easier way out: Stay accessible.

Warm-Up Exercises

Your own working methods will evolve as you go, but I have used my plan of getting started each day for many years. Here is how it goes. Start at the same time each working day, as though you have a job in some place of business—as in truth you do. Each morning I get out of bed rather

Autry Dye
Artist
Gulf Breeze, Florida

If only everyone could go to work as easily and happily as Autry Dye! Dye just walks through her breakfast room into a gallery and studio she and her husband built in the garage. Here she tells how they created her space and what it's meant to her career—and her life.

Q. *Autry, you have created a unique studio/gallery out of a portion of your garage and no one would know from the street that it was a studio or from the house that it was a garage. How did this all come about?*

A. For most of my married life I had taken some small, out-of-the-family's-way space for my art. The area was usually shared with the washing machine, lawn mower, guest bedroom/sewing room, etc. There was hardly space for my drafting table, let alone any new equipment that I was acquiring. My husband also realized that I needed more space. Since the two-car garage was seldom used for its intended purpose, it seemed the logical place.

Q. *Your space works beautifully but it does not detract from the resale value of the house. The garage could be restored in no time, yet the studio looks so permanent and well built from inside the house. How did you accomplish that in remodeling?*

A. One of the most important things we did was to raise the studio floor to the level of the house floor. The floor level is what integrates the studio space so well that the house does not look remodeled.

Q. *Have you found your space large enough for all your present needs?*

A. Since I do all facets of my·work—the creating, mat cutting, framing, and shipping—I could use more space. Especially since I even teach small watercolor classes in my studio. I can accommodate five or six students at a time. Students seem to like to come to my studio. They have access to a great deal of resource in my studio, the schedule is not rigid, there's coffee in the kitchen, and there are no failing grades here.

Q. *You've talked about the studio aspect of your space, now how about your gallery?*

A. My gallery is by appointment only, so that my neighbors are never disturbed. The same space I use for working and teaching is also gallery space. Sometimes it takes a while to make the transition from work area to display, but I have a twenty-foot wall on one side of my room that is covered with pegboard and holds my work. There is a comfortable chair and table in one corner and whenever a prospective client is arriving, I put on some pleasant background "music to buy paintings by."

When I started selling my work in art shows, I needed a business license and a tax

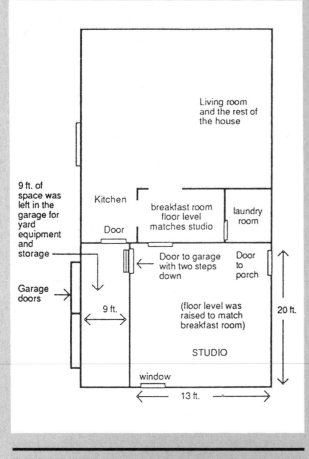

Living room
and the rest of
the house

9 ft. of
space was
left in the
garage for
yard
equipment
and
storage

Kitchen

Door

breakfast room
floor level
matches studio

laundry
room

Door to garage
with two steps
down

Door
to
porch

Garage
doors

9 ft.

(floor level was
raised to match
breakfast room)

20 ft.

STUDIO

window

13 ft.

This floor plan shows how Dye's garage-cum-studio is part of the house, yet gives her the privacy she needs to work.

number and then it was just a short step to selling work from my home.

I have my own business accounts at the bank and am set up to accept charge cards. When someone expresses an interest in a painting, but lacks funds, accepting charge cards may make the sale. Sometimes, I make it even easier by accepting layaway. I've done this many times and then shipped the painting after it is paid for. I usually require one-third to one-fourth down, paid monthly.

Q. *Do you think guests coming to your home ever feel put on the spot to purchase artwork because you have a gallery here?*
A. I hope not. I don't think anyone could ever say I'm a high-pressure salesperson. When we have guests, the connecting door between my studio and the living area is always closed. I do not take anyone into the gallery unless they ask to see my work, but I have found that most people are really curious about the whole process of creating.

Q. *What do you feel are the advantages and disadvantages of having your professional space in your home?*
A. Well, for me, at this time in my life, I want and need to make money. And the big advantage is that I have freedom to work whatever hours I choose without having to leave my home—say at midnight when the painting urge is on me. I can do laundry or cook while waiting for some process to complete itself. I like being at home. The disadvantage is that you do have distractions, if you allow them to intrude and, frankly, I lack discipline and know I might get more creative work done if my studio was away from home. However, the idea of a rigid schedule where I went to work every day at 9 a.m. and returned at 5 p.m. would soon drive me crazy. Somehow during each day I manage to get some creative work done and I get what I do require—a certain place to be, without interruptions, where I can be alone to concentrate on serious painting whether the actual brush is to paper or I'm just thinking about the subject at hand and how I want to present it.

Q. *Have you ever had serious trouble with customers coming into your home?*
A. I try to prevent that by making my ap-

pointments in the right way. Each artist has to decide what is safe. If I don't know a person, I try to get a reference before opening my home. You might feel you want to do what another artist I know does—always meet a stranger at a public place before inviting that client into a secluded home situation.

Q. *I know you exhibit in galleries, too. How does your advertising budget for your home studio/gallery compare with the commission you pay other galleries?*

A. Favorably. I don't object to paying a gallery commission if the gallery is working well for me. The exposure provided by a good gallery should offset the commission. My main reason for having a gallery at home is not to try to save commissions, but to have convenience. I find that, this year, I have spent more on my own advertising than I would have on gallery commissions. I did some special things like paying for my space in a published book on artists in my area, but the publishers gave me a wonderful amount of tear sheets of my section done in the form of a brochure about me (see page 41), so it all comes out in the wash.

Q. *What advice do you have for artists wishing to be in your situation?*

A. That they take a very critical look at the existing space in their home. I feel most homes offer alternate space usage. Ask yourself if you really need a separate family room and living room. How much do you use your basement or attic? It's not easy, but if your desire to have a work area of your very own is strong enough you will give up some other space. Of course, it helps to have a cooperative family.

early, because I'm a slow starter. My work day does not begin until nine, but I like to get up about six-thirty, so I can enjoy a leisurely cup of coffee, the view, or the morning show on TV. This is also a time for communicating with my soul, for planning big things to come. Sometimes it's pure daydreaming, yet important and constructive. It's true that what you think you are, you will become. So, in the morning I spend some time enjoying the successful artist that I am. Then, when the hands of the clock reach 8:45, I have finished breakfast and am ready to get my mind in gear for creating. I don't start on a masterpiece right away. My favorite way of warming up is to do what I call blind squiggles.

Blind squiggles are designs done with eyes shut. First, take a sheet of typing paper and draw about six rectangles on it. Don't let the rectangles touch one another. Their size will be about 2 x 3 inches. You can control your hand better working in that size. Now, with your eyes open, place a ballpoint pen (the kind with a long barrel for easy handling) in an advantageous design spot inside one of the rectangles. This means you will *not* place your pen point in the exact center of the rectangle nor in the center of any of the quadrants of the rectangle. All of those spots are awkward for good designs. A good spot to place your pen is just a little to the right of the center of the rectangle and just below or above an imaginary line dividing the rectangle in half. Start here the first time. Now close your eyes and start to move your pen.

Make any kind of marks that you want, all the while keeping the size of the rectangle in mind with your eyes closed. Don't peek. Just make marks without lifting your pen from the paper. If you are in the mood for straight strong strokes, do them; if you prefer oval or rounded organic shapes, go with them. Continue to move your pen for several seconds so that you build up some marks, one over the other, keeping your eyes closed. Don't look at your squiggle yet.

Now, as you get ready to end this squiggle, do

a few thrusts of the pen in a different direction or shape. All the time you are doing this, you should be thinking of the size and shape of your original rectangle. Now, as you open your eyes you'll be surprised to see what you have done. Keep these designs for future reference.

In your first one you may find you have gone out over the edges, or you made your design much smaller or larger than you thought. That's okay. Look at this design upside down, then sideways. What comes out? What could you turn it into? If you don't feel that the design is good, don't try to correct it. Do another. If you have gone out of the boundaries, try to stay more contained the next time. Concentrate harder on your rectangular space with your eyes closed. If you open your eyes while squiggling, you destroy the communication that you have set up with your subconscious.

Do one design after the other and analyze later. It is important to analyze only the marks inside the rectangle. Keep a bottle of typewriter correction fluid at hand to "white out" all the marks that extend over the borders. Look at the designs at all angles—upside down, sideways—to see which way each design works best.

Save all these squiggles. When you don't know what to paint or you need some inspiration on work you have been assigned, bring out a bunch of your "squiggles" and let your imagination wander over them. One will spark your imagination for a new approach to whatever kind of painting you must do that day. Your squiggles serve several purposes. They keep you in a running conversation with yourself; they provide designs for future paintings; they help you get started into a productive painting day—get your mind and hands working together; and they tell you much about your mood and what you need to conquer in your design thinking. Good paintings can grow from these squiggles.

As soon as I have put in one half-hour or so at squiggles, I go on to put in a full morning of painting. The squiggles have warmed me up, and I'm off—my hands, head, and heart all working in unison. I save today's squiggles for future use and get on to the work at hand.

My rule for beginning a painting is to find a squiggle and a design plan, then to follow a good definition of a painting. This is my favorite definition: A painting is an arrangement of areas of color, within another given area, so as to produce a desired effect. That's so easy it's hard!

Knowing When to Stop

When it comes to ending the painting, we all need some help. Artists have a joke about what it takes to produce a good painting: One artist to paint it and one to say stop. You can be your own backup artist if you follow some simple rules. First, stop working on the painting as soon as you give out the slightest sigh of boredom, or as soon as you don't know what to do next. Put the painting away for awhile . . . an hour or a day. After that, decide how to finish it by asking yourself:

- Does the painting check out by the "four-quarter method"?
- Does the painting have a warm or a cool dominance?
- Does the painting contain three values: light, medium, and dark?
- Where does the lightest light meet the darkest dark?

Let's consider each question thoroughly.

First: the four-quarter method. Tape your painting up on the wall. Stand back about ten feet, or as far away as is comfortable for viewing. Take two index cards (one in each hand) and hold them up at arm's length. Allow the lower left corner of the right card to barely touch the upper right corner of the left card. Close one eye so that you see two separate quarters of the painting. Concentrate on one quadrant at a time. Now, simply decide if that quarter "looks good." Is it exciting? Is it boring? If it's boring you will know it and you will know it's bad. After you

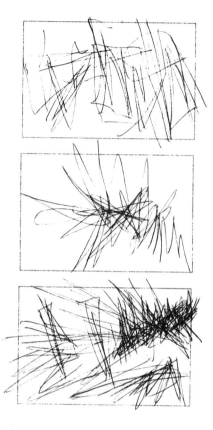

"Bird Landing on Fence," Edna Wagner Piersol, 30 x 40 inches, watercolor.

I use squiggles done with my eyes closed to start my creative juices flowing, so that my painting time is productive and I have designs for the future. The bottom squiggle provided the basic design for "Bird Landing on Fence."

have concentrated on one quarter, do the same with the other. Then reverse the cards and repeat the process until you have analyzed all four quarters. To find out what "good quadrants" should look like, go to a museum and look at famous paintings. Especially look at the works of the Old Masters. See how exciting different sections of many of the pictures appear. If you can't get to museums, use reproductions of famous paintings in books.

Second: warm or cool dominance in a painting. It's risky to try to make a painting work with one-half cool color and one-half warm color. It's much easier to quickly add a little warm or cool to tip the scales in one direction or the other. Usually, this will pull the painting together effectively. Such dominance, although slight, does much to create a feeling of unity. (Study the paintings in the gallery on pages 107-117 to learn more about warm/cool dominance.)

The third question is probably the simplest to see and the hardest to control. Does your painting have three distinct values? If your painting is weak in contrasting values, it will lack impact. That may be the effect you want. If so, okay. But, often a careful analysis shows that a clear definition of three distinct values is what the composition needs for unity and structure. Once again, tape the painting to the wall and stand back. Squint your eyes until they are barely open and you will see the painting in simplified value. If you feel you can't divorce your thinking from the painting's subject matter, turn the painting upside down—a good thing to do while answering all of the questions.

The fourth question to answer is where do your darkest darks touch your lightest lights? Where they touch will produce a strong visual attraction, a center of interest. Be sure this is the area you want the viewer to notice. If these areas are in the wrong places, it is often easy to make adjustments by changing some light colors. By altering the value in a white area, you can diminish its importance. For example, if the light area is on a white house, the house can be painted light blue or gray, or given a tint of any color, because white reflects all colors. Many artists have a fondness for making the sky a light value in landscapes. Often this creates an area of strong light against dark all along the horizon, tree or roof line, or whatever. The eye is drawn there, trapped in an unimportant path along that portion of the painting. I've found a medium value has definite advantages for skies. See what happens to the dynamism of your landscape with a darker sky.

When you have answered these four questions to your satisfaction, you have finished a painting with assurance. Never again will you need to wonder if a painting is done.

Painting Commissions

Make commission work reward your soul as well as your pocketbook. How do you do that? We all hate to do what someone else tells us to do. Most

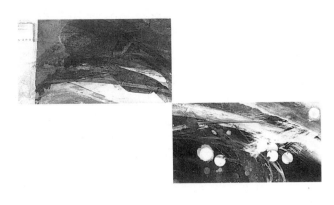

Barbara Gresham's painting, "Kimono," checks out beautifully using the four-quarter method. Each quadrant has an exciting design. (Turn to page 112 to see the complete painting.)

of us are a cantankerous lot. We can't help it. We have highly individual personalities. The trick to making commission work rewarding is to look for something in your client's thoughts that interests you. If he wants you to do a painting of his favorite cow, how can *you* become interested? Well, what does interest you? Color? Then become fascinated by how you can produce interesting colors on that cow. Design? What kind of squiggles have you produced that can be applied to the animal? Your client doesn't care *where* you place the cow, just so it looks like *his* cow. He will be impressed when you create a dynamic design.

I repeat my favorite definition of a painting usually attributed to an unknown artist: *A painting is an arrangement of areas of color, within another given area, so as to produce a desired effect.* Other versions end in "greatest degree of emotion" or "so as to produce beauty." But I think "to produce a desired effect" is the best ending. The "meat" of the definition is the beginning: *A painting is an arrangement of areas of color. That is what you must abide by when you paint.* You are not a camera or a recorder. You are speaking a new language. You are arranging areas of color. Sometimes you might want to change the definition to "a *drawing* is an arrangement of lines, values," etc. or "a sketch is an arrangement of areas of lights and darks," etc. The definition will help you think about what you are doing as a process, a means to an end, and not a copying exercise. *You* are the artist. *You* are speaking to the world. The best way to communicate is to let out your subconscious. To do this, use squiggles, doodles, or other methods of your own. Then translate through paint. When you are speaking, it doesn't matter what the subject is, as long as you speak your own way. Your clients will only love you more for being individual.

Once, while I was in Florida, I received a call from a young woman in Kentucky. She had bought my paintings before and now wanted me to do an abstract to go above her couch. We all know the "couch-size painting" jokes. But why

"House Interior, Ocean Grove" Edna Wagner Piersol, 30 x 42 inches, watercolor.

The customer who commissioned this piece asked me to present her home my own way. I used features of several rooms to form a sort of collage of the most interesting aspects—the customer had not known what to expect, but she loved it!

not? (By the way, 30 x 40 inches is a good "couch-size" painting.) Why shouldn't a client ask for a "couch-size" painting? Michelangelo was constantly asked for a "cathedral-size" painting. My client proceeded to tell me the colors she wanted: deep blue, apricot, a little yellow, deep rust, parrot green. Oh, my. She sent me a swatch of her couch material and a color chip of her "off-white" wall.

I can see your hands flying up in horror. Where is the originality? Doesn't creativity count at all? Certainly it does. You can be as creative with someone else's ideas as you are with your own, perhaps even more so. The challenge is greater. Michelangelo almost always worked with someone else's desires in mind. Where was his originality? Don't I wish I had as

much as he had? So, after my commission call, I went to work.

That dear woman had trusted me enough to commission me over the phone, certain that I could produce a painting that would please both of us. She said she wanted an original Piersol.

I let my imagination roam. I took out my squiggles. I thought of blues and apricots and off-white. Parrot green? Some bright white might add interest. She had not confined me to her colors; she just wanted each of hers used. My thoughts kept returning to the ocean which I could hear in the background. I found a squiggle that suited.

Digging out some magazines and old brochures from other artists, I selected pictures produced in grays—no color. I cut out sections of them in the values I wanted: light, medium, dark. I didn't cut out objects; just sections of tone. Then I tore those sections into pieces that fit my squiggle design pattern, keeping it all small enough to fit into a little design about 3½ x 5 inches. I find it easier to create designs by working small and without a brush in my hand. My brush is for rendering large flows of paint on the finished product. My fascination with what the brush does sometimes hinders my design sense.

After I had my little "paper piece" design, I pasted it down and made three photocopies of it—one for my client and two for me (a spare). If my little pasted-up design came apart, nothing was lost. All the design planning was done in grays, black, and white; no color. When satisfied with the design, I went to work, faithfully transferring it to the correct proportion on a large piece of gesso-coated masonite.

Was I creating? I certainly was. My painting was totally my own. My client felt she had participated and indeed she had, but the painting was mine, all mine. No matter how uninteresting a commission may seem, it becomes exciting as your own creativity takes over. Your work plan is the means by which you channel and use your creativity.

Discipline—simply making yourself work—is the key to success. The way to do that is to set up a work plan and stick to it religiously. Do whatever it takes to force yourself to work. Starving is a good incentive. If you arrange your life so that you have to survive on what your paintbrush produces, you have given yourself the best present you will ever receive: incentive. Incentive breeds discipline; discipline breeds success.

"Old Portland Home," Edna Wagner Piersol, 28 x 36 inches, watercolor on tissue paper coated with wax.

This is one of eight paintings I did for the mayor's office of Louisville, Kentucky. In painting this series, I tried to combine the "official" view of the city—famous places like Churchill Downs—with some of the day-to-day life of the city, which this painting represents.

CHAPTER FOUR

Creating a Successful Image

What is your image? It is how people perceive you. Create a successful image for yourself; build it from your credentials.

Your Résumé

Start your image with a *résumé* (sometimes called a vitae or bio). You will give this to prospective clients and other people who ask for information about you. Prepare your résumé when you have enough credits to fill about three-quarters of a page (they can be double spaced and stretched a little).

Choose the most exciting things you have done. State them in a way that will impress. Be positive. For instance, don't say, "I taught a few classes in watercolor at an art center." Instead, say, "Instructed watercolor classes at the North Hills Art Center." Get some professional help, either from résumé agencies (listed in the phone book) or books on the subject (available at public libraries).

An artist's résumé needs to be different from a corporation executive's, but the main rule is still that the résumé should be professional — state professional facts in a professional way.

I've put together a rather bad artist's résumé made up of excerpts from résumés sent to me for critique to show you some common mistakes. Many of these résumés are also poorly typed with uneven (light and dark) letters — that's very bad. It is best to have your résumé typeset or prepared by an expert on an electric typewriter or word processor.

This résumé doesn't play up the artist's strong points. Instead, it makes her sound like an amateur.

```
Resume of Jenny Paintwell


Height — 5' 2"
Weight — 105 lbs.
Health — excellent


I am a 38 year old house wife and mother of two boys ages 9
and 12.
In 1983, I began to paint in oils as a hobby, as I do not have a
degree in art.
I paint landscapes and flowers.
Have been selling paintings since 1984.
Taught art classes at Fallsworth Art Center, 1986-87.
Taught art classes for children, ages 6 to 8, in Bible School at
St. Mark's Lutheran Church, Fallsworth, VA.

EDUCATION IN ART
First watercolor course from Sue Splash at Fallsworth Art Center.
Workshops and classes at the Adult Education Center of Schenley
High School.  Also classes from Jane Artteach 1983 - present.

EXHIBITS
Mercer Co Fair, juryed Art Show, Mercer, PA 1985
St. Catherines Folk Society Art Show, Suffolk, VA 1985
Virginia State Fair Art Exhibit, Richmond, VA 1986
Jubilee Art Show, Fairfax, VA 1987
Virginia State Fair Art Exhibit, Richmond, VA 1987

AWARDS
Honorable Mention, Mercer Co. Fair 1985.
Out of two paintings entered was awarded First Place, Landscape
and Still Life, St. Catherine's Folk Society Art Show, 1985.
Third Place, Still Life, Virginia State Fair, 1986.
```

Critique

Most of the information in the résumé is good but it has been arranged badly. Also, it contains

```
COLLECTIONS: (Selected)
Mr. and Mrs. Jack Public, Fairfax, VA
Office of Ms. Ann Storm, Alexandria, VA
Mr. and Mrs. Jan Allen, Fairfax, VA
Mr. and Mrs. John Smith, Richmond, VA
Mr. and Mrs. Irby Windes, Tampa, FL
Ms. Sue Anderson, Bethesda, MD
Mr. H. Edmunds, Tampa, FL
Mr. J. M. Jones, Fairfax, VA
Mr. and Mrs. Allen Drew, Richmond, VA
Mr. and Mrs. Forge Park, Richmond, VA
The Alright Tobacco Co., Tampa FL
Fallsworth Public Library
```

some facts that aren't important.

I seriously doubt that people who buy art care if the artist is 5'2" and weighs 105 lbs. They may care that she is a 38-year-old housewife and mother of two boys, but that should not be one of the first things called to their attention in the résumé. Interesting facts like those need to be placed under some applicable heading like *Personal* at the end of the résumé. Your *name and address and phone number* should be on *everything* you send out and it should go at the top of each page of your résumé.

Don't ever use the word "hobby" in any description of your main occupation as this artist has done in the introduction. I understand the "problem" of not having a degree because I don't have one either, but I have learned, through much hard work and analysis of my own feelings, that I must not dwell on that or apologize by constantly announcing the fact to the world. If I work to be the best I can be, truth will win out, as they say. The same is true for you.

Under EDUCATION: Get to the point. Just say "self-taught plus private studies in watercolor" (or whatever). Don't use a teacher's name unless that teacher's name is a household word. It would be good if you could get a course or two from some college or university to list here.

Under EXHIBITS: There is a misspelled word—*juryed* is wrong—*juried* is the correct spelling. Spelling, grammar, and sentence construction are extremely important in a résumé so always check them very carefully. Then have another person check them.

Under AWARDS: State things simply, accentuating the best. Begin with first-place awards and then go to second, third, and honorable mention. In this résumé (which is short compared to that of a more experienced artist), the AWARDS section should come first, and then EXHIBITS, COLLECTIONS, EDUCATION, and PERSONAL. Always hit the public with the best you have to offer first. Awards get their attention. If you had studied under Picasso, you might list

education first.

Under COLLECTIONS: I like the use of the term *selected*. It should be placed after EXHIBITIONS and AWARDS as well as after COLLECTIONS. This artist's list of collections would not be impressive to the general public who would not know the names of most of these collectors. At this stage of her career, however, these names add length and interest to the résumé. If the list gets any longer with unknown collectors' names, though, this section should probably just say, "The Alright Tobacco Co., Tampa, Florida, the Fallsworth Public Library, Fallsworth, Virginia, and public and private collections throughout Virginia, Maryland, and Florida."

You'll be surprised at how impressed people are with a good printed résumé. Sometimes it amuses me how much people give credit to the printed word. On page 38 is a corrected résumé for Jenny Paintwell so you can compare.

Other Mistakes

Here is another common mistake from the résumé of a different artist who does have a degree.

EDUCATION	Good Hope University—Physical Education
	Individual study with:
	Janet Teach and Cobb Brush
	Workshops with:
	Paul Brown
TEACHING POSITIONS	Physical Ed., Jefferson High School, Marks, Indiana

Your education should always be mentioned, but since this is your artist résumé, make sure the general public is really aware of the art part of your education. If you studied or taught something that is unrelated to art, like Physical Education, be sure that in your art résumé, you list other accomplishments that relate to art.

The corrected résumé follows.

EDUCATION   Good Hope University — Physical
Education
PAINTING AND DESIGN — Individual
study with:
Janet Teach and Cobb Brush,
1983 and 1984
WATERCOLOR WORKSHOPS with:
Paul Brown, 1984 and 1985

EDUCATION   Art Institute of Pittsburgh
Independent studies in Painting and
Design, Art History, Psychology, and
Graphology at:
Carnegie-Mellon University, Pitts-
burgh; University of Pittsburgh; J. B.
Speed Museum, Louisville, Ken-
tucky; and Troy State University,
Hurlburt Field, Florida Campus.

Even when your whole education has been art related, always use it to its best advantage on your résumé. My main art education was completed at a commercial art school, so I've also used the names of the colleges where I've done short studies. Part of my résumé reads:

In this résumé, the artist makes the most of her background by placing personal information below her more impressive credentials about awards, exhibits, and education.

My career has become so varied with writing and other marketing activities that I've broken my résumé up into categories, so that I don't have to include all the pages for every client. When I'm trying for a one-person exhibit at a museum, I don't send the page about market research and advertising. I've got an introductory page that gives some of my most impressive credentials and establishes who I am. Then I have separate pages

```
RESUME
Jenny Paintwell
733 Indian Trail, Fallsworth, VA 32541
(412) 237-3380


Artist Jenny Paintwell specializes in oil paintings of flowers
and landscapes.

AWARDS: (Selected)
First Place, Landscape and Still Life, St. Catherine's Folk
Society Art Show, 1985
Third Place, Still Life, Virginia State Fair, 1986
Honorable Mention, Mercer Co. Fair 1985

EXHIBITS: (Selected)
Mercer Co. Fair, juried Art Show, Mercer, PA 1985
St. Catherine's Folk Society Art Show, Suffolk, VA 1985
Virginia State Fair Art Exhibit, Richmond, VA 1986, 1987
Jubilee Art Show, Fairfax, VA 1987

COLLECTIONS: (Selected)
The Alright Tobacco Co., Tampa, FL
Fallsworth Public Library, Fallsworth, VA
Mr. and Mrs. Jack Public, Fairfax, VA
Office of Ms. Ann Storm, Alexandria, VA
Mr. and Mrs. Jan Allen, Fairfax, VA
Mr. and Mrs. John Smith, Richmond, VA
Mr. and Mrs. Irby Windes, Tampa, FL
Ms. Sue Anderson, Bethesda, MD
Mr. H. Edmunds, Tampa, FL
Mr. J. M. Jones, Fairfax, VA
Mr. and Mrs. Allen Drew, Richmond, VA
Mr. and Mrs. Forge Park, Richmond, VA

EDUCATION:
Self taught plus adult education classes in Design and private
studies in Watercolor.
```

```
PERSONAL:
Born Washington D.C., 1947
Married to Paul Paintwell, chemical engineer for Locke Chemicals,
Fallsworth, VA
Mother of two boys ages 9 and 12

TEACHING POSITIONS:
Fallsworth Art Center — Watercolor Classes, 1986-87
Bible School at St. Mark's Lutheran Church, Fallsworth, VA — Art
classes for children ages 6 to 8.
```

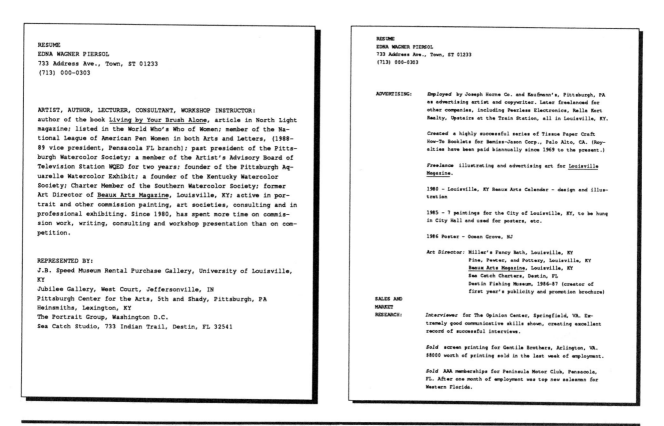

Artists whose credentials are lengthy can tailor their résumés to the particular audience by preparing a separate page for each area of expertise. A general introduction page like the one shown here can be accompanied by other pages showing accomplishments in different areas, such as the page from my résumé on my advertising background.

that give details about different aspects of my career, like the page on advertising and marketing shown here.

There is another section about fine arts and one on writing. I can send one to five pages to any client, accentuating whatever phase of my career I choose.

At the *top of each page of the résumé* is the heading:

RÉSUMÉ
EDNA WAGNER PIERSOL
733 Address Ave., Town, ST 01233
(713)000 - 0303

Artists often need several different formats

for the info on their résumés—sometimes a newspaper reporter will ask for feature story-type information—and at other times a prospective employer or client wants just hard facts. I find my way of organizing a résumé very workable. If a category needs more than one page (such as fine arts does for me), I place a line stating "Fine Arts, continued—" just under the heading of the second page and third page, etc., of that category.

Other Printed Pieces

You will need other printed pieces besides your résumé: business cards, brochures on your expertise in a special area such as illustrations or portraits, and mailing cards for general use to keep reminding the world that you exist. You should also have letterhead stationery indicating the kind of artist you are. All of these pieces should be exciting and used to spread your talent around the world.

Your *business card* must have good design. Nothing will defeat your purpose more quickly than a card that looks as if it were made by an amateur artist. If you are using a picture of a painting on the card, use one that you have seen reduced to size. Be sure it holds up and looks as good after reduction as it did before. Don't trust a printer to tell you it will look good; he's not an artist. I'm a firm believer in specialists. Find a good designer for all of your printed pieces; she knows what will work. Your business card should contain your name and address, plus the word *artist* or *illustrator* (some title to indicate that you are an artist), and your phone number. Let the card be arty, but keep it simple and effective.

Brochures are very useful. I have two, one for workshops and another for portraits. Once every two years, I go over my brochures and have new ones made. From time to time I make up short runs of a brochure for a quick project like my Ocean Avenue series. Never stint on these. It's better to print a good one every couple of years than to try to run off sloppy, mimeographed ones that do more harm than good.

A good brochure is one that contains some selling information. In other words, it is a sophisticated, strongly designed advertisement about you and your work. In it you will need a few photos of your work. Strongly contrasted black-and-white shots of your finished paintings are effective. You should also have a photo of yourself and you must include an address and phone number or the brochure will be useless. It isn't a good idea to include prices since they change. Instead, use a separate price sheet that can be printed more cheaply.

My *mailing cards* are multipurpose. I use them for notes to friends, as enclosures in letters,

Professional-looking printed pieces, such as Dawn Weimer's stationery and Keets Rivers' business card, give customers the impression that you're serious about your art.

Marge Alderson's brochure is an excellent example of an all-purpose mailing piece. Inside are a photo of her, her credentials, and another painting.

or to hand to clients. Whenever I finish a painting that I especially like or one of my paintings receives an award, I commemorate it by having a 5 x 7-inch black-and-white glossy photo made. Glossy photos are better for reproduction and can be reduced for use on any card size. I then have picture postcards printed with my newest painting.

Printing Procedures

For those of you who have never had any printing done, I'll take you through the basic processes.

First, you'll need a layout, a plan drawn to the actual size of the printing. Let's say that you have a 5 x 7-inch photo of one of your paintings, and you want to use it on a 3 x 5-inch mailing card. Of course it will not fit, but your printer can reduce it. How do you know what size to tell him to reduce it to? There is a simple way. Draw a 5 x 7-inch rectangle. Then draw a diagonal line through the rectangle, from bottom left to top right.

If your painting is horizontal, it needs to be reduced to about two-and-a-half inches high in order to fit inside the card and allow a little margin. How much space will be left for printing? How wide will the reduced picture be? To find out, measure up the left side of your rectangle to two-and-a-half inches. Now draw a straight line, parallel to the base line, over to the diagonal line and another line straight down from the spot where the lines meet to the bottom of the rectangle. You now have the exact size of the reduction. Place the little rectangle on your layout, exactly where you want the picture. You'll now see the space left for your printing.

You will be able to tell from the printer's sample book what typeface looks good, but it is another matter to choose a type-point size. The printer will know how small the point size has to be in order to get all of your wording to fit. If the type looks too small to you, you will have to eliminate some of the words. Let simplicity of

Autry Dye's lovely four-color mailing piece was a bonus when she allowed her artwork to be published in a magazine and in return was able to have these printed at a greatly reduced cost. A photograph of Dye and some background information are printed on the reverse.

design be the star; the fewer words you use, the larger they can be.

It will help you to know something about how a photograph is printed. In order to reproduce it, the printer must first shoot a negative of your photo. This negative is shot through a screen that breaks up your picture into little dots of various sizes to create halftone effects. Look at a newspaper picture with a magnifying glass and you will see the dots. (For a newspaper, the dots must be quite coarse.)

Knowing how the process works can help you to choose photographs of your work, ones that have good contrast. To decide what areas or fine lines might be lost in the printing process, squint at the photo with your eyes half closed. Anything you don't see is not likely to show up on the printed piece.

Only pictures with grays in them need screens. Line drawings do not require screens for

I use two types of portfolios. The smaller one, briefcase size (shown at top), travels easily and can be used for making presentations to potential clients. The larger one is big enough to carry original, unframed work.

to get two hundred brochures as one hundred, and probably as expensive to get ten as one hundred. At five hundred and more, you should receive further price breaks.

This basic printing information should be used as a guide to make you feel more confident about what you are doing, but I can't stress enough the advantages of professional help. Save yourself a lot of grief by finding a good photographer, printer, and graphic designer, and make use of all of them. Even if you are a graphic designer, another designer can present you better. A surgeon does not operate on himself.

Presentation Tools

Once your printed pieces are available, you'll need some other tools before you are ready to make a presentation to a potential client.

A *briefcase-size portfolio* can be bought at most art supply stores. Mine is the 11 x 14-inch size. In it I have several 8 x 10-inch color photographs of paintings. Those photos are expensive, but I have as many paintings as possible photographed. Also in the briefcase are some small samples of drawings, newspaper clippings, and testimonial letters—all things that will impress clients. The briefcase has a pocket on either side to hold my brochures. As long as that portfolio is in my car, I'm ready at any moment to make a presentation.

I also have a *large portfolio* for paintings, although I don't carry it with me at all times. When a client has expressed an interest in seeing actual work, I pack it carefully. I make the paintings look as good as possible without frames by using good-looking mats and a foam-core backing on each one to keep it straight. Each painting is wrapped in clear vinyl. This can be bought by the yard in the housewares department of a discount store. The vinyl I like is the kind used in making tablecloths, etc., since it is more supple than acetate. Also, it's usually cheaper. Whatever you use, the portfolio contents must be neat and very

printing; therefore, they are cheaper to reproduce. The printing of color photographs requires a separate screen for each basic color. To achieve a full-color effect, you need four screened negatives—red, yellow, blue, and black—and four printing runs through the press. That gets expensive. A way to get color into your printed pieces without a lot of extra cost is by using a colored ink for the entire printing. You can also use colored paper and colored ink—two colors for the price of one.

Printers usually offer price breaks with larger quantities, so you may find it is almost as cheap well organized.

Sometimes a slide viewer and 35mm color transparencies of your paintings work better than taking the actual work. I have a book for slides with clear vinyl pages containing twenty pockets per page. The slides can be organized according to subject and the pages held up to the light in a client's office so he can quickly see what he likes. The slides he chooses can then be shown on the small viewer you carry with you. Never make a client supply any equipment, such as a slide projector, but at the same time, never carry so much paraphernalia into his office as to be obtrusive. Be neat and well organized.

Telephoning Clients

At this point you should be ready for your big presentation. You have found a client by advertising or, perhaps, you are going to make what salespeople dub a "cold call." Let's take it from the top and walk through this one together.

Pick up the Yellow Pages of the phone directory and look at the ads for interior decorators. (Select one who can afford a large ad.) I've found that a good time of day to phone decorators is four in the afternoon. They are back in their offices and finished with clients for the day. This is another kind of research you have to do—finding good psychological times to approach people, but another book could be written on that.

Now, go ahead, dial her number.

("Jacob's Interiors.") It is a secretary or assistant.

"Hello, my name is (Edna Wagner Piersol); I am an artist and I've been associated with (Norcross Gallery in Cleveland) for a long time. I'm not a Sunday painter."

It is important to let the potential client know that you are a professional. In your introduction say the most exciting thing you can about yourself as an artist. Don't be shy. Say loud and clear, "I have recently won an award in the (Gulf Coast Art Show)," or "I'm listed in (*Who's Who of Art-*

ists)." Stick to facts. Don't make up anything, but this stage is terribly important, so it is not the time to be modest either. Don't even think of saying something silly like "I call myself an artist." *Pick one or two of your most impressive accomplishments and state them.* Then say, "I am calling to inquire if your company ever purchases paintings directly from artists."

You will save a lot of time and effort by finding out this crucial point immediately. If you get a "yes" answer to your inquiry, you can then make an appointment to see the decorator and show your wares. If they say "no," go on to the next decorator in the Yellow Pages.

In-Person Calls

Sometimes instead of a "cold" telephone call I make a "cold" personal call, and these are always well thought out. I check out the shop in advance to determine if I think my paintings would go well with its other merchandise. In this case I have my big portfolio in the car packed with paintings that I think this particular client may like. But I do not take it into the shop until the introductions are over.

I walk in with my portfolio of photos, etc., in one hand and a printed brochure in the other. I go so far as to fold the brochure in such a way that a photo will be sure to catch any interested eye. Be aware that you probably won't see "the boss" at this moment. It will be the assistant, but walk in smiling and say, "Hello, I'm (Edna Wagner Piersol). I'm an artist."

Extend the printed brochure saying, "I've been selling to (Smith Decorators in Cleveland) for quite a while and I want to expand my market. Do you ever buy work directly from artists?"

When you are talking to an assistant, be just as friendly as you will be when you finally meet the boss. You want to impress him so that when he gives your brochure and message to "Ms. Big," she is in your corner already. Tell the assis-

Eric Piersol
Manager, Furniture/Collectibles Store
Lexington, Kentucky

Eric Piersol, who happens to be the author's son, is the manager of Heinsmiths, a fine collectibles store in Lexington, Kentucky. His advice to artists wishing to sell their work to decorators follows.

Q. *What kind of paintings would you be most likely to buy directly from artists?*

A. We have purchased all types; however, the more traditional pieces such as landscapes, seascapes, still lifes, seem to do best. Oils and watercolors or acrylics seem to be the most preferred media. Unfortunately, people in the design business usually look for color first, then how it and the subject or style will fit a particular room or scheme, not at art for art's sake.

Q. *How would you prefer an artist contact you — by mail, phone, or in person?*

A. Personally I prefer contact by mail or phone first, to set up an appointment. My time is extremely valuable and I prefer to devote segments usefully. An appointment also allows me a planned amount of time to view the works and make planned decisions as to purchases, especially after I am familiar with an artist and his or her work.

Q. *Do you prefer an artist to show you framed paintings or would you rather buy them unframed? When paintings are framed, what kind of frames are best for the decorating business?*

A. It is best for us to purchase unframed paintings and frame them. This way we are sure that the frame complements the painting as well as the room in which it will hang. The type of matting and the color or combination of colors of the mats are also important.

As far as what kind of frames are best for the design business, a great deal depends on the painting itself. A frame's main purpose is to form a border between the art and the environment. In addition it must complement the painting and the decor which it becomes a part of. One would not put a seventeenth-century Dutch oil of flowers in a chrome frame nor would one put a Peter Max in a very ornate gold molding.

Q. *What kind of presentation by artists impresses you and perhaps causes you to buy from them?*

A. A personal presentation of an hour or so with a portfolio of their work. I prefer to see the actual work rather than photographs.

Q. *How good is the market for original art in your kind of business?*

A. We break it down into categories: size, media, subject, color ... not necessarily in that order but all are important. Unfortunately, unless you are in the upper end of the design business, the marketability hinges on the above and one other big factor . . . *price!* Unless you are in the end of the business in which your clients are looking for investments in art as well as interior design, "art" has very little to do with it. Otherwise it must fit in general to the regional taste and be in the price point at which the dealer can buy it from you and resell it allowing him a 40 to 50 percent profit. For example, in our area an average-size (25 x 30 inches), traditional oil painting, framed, sells well at between $600 and $800. We would need to be able to purchase this for $240 to $320.

Q. *From your contact with other decorating and furniture businesses in other parts of the country, what do you feel are the chances of artists selling to decorators? How should an artist go about exploring this market?*

A. As I said, the price is a big factor, assuming that the artist is good and that the subjects and media fit in with the regional tastes or the prevalent design themes of the area: traditional, Southwest, eclectic, contemporary, neoclassic, Oriental . . . all are usually present in any given area in lieu of our "global" economy. However, there is usually one which is prevalent. Learn which scheme is the prevalent one and study which art goes best with these schemes. Then approach the design studios and furniture stores. You might even suggest custom work, done with specific clients in mind, specific colors, themes, etc. There are also several firms that market art at the seasonal furniture and accessory markets. They usually sign artists on to work exclusively for them.

tant that you would like to see the owner or manager, and if you can't see her that day, find out when would be a good time to call for an appointment.

When you are finally granted an interview with a new client, it should go like this:

Walk in once again with your briefcase portfolio under your arm and a brochure in your hand. You should have the slide projector and slides neatly packed in a small bag, your portfolio in the car waiting.

"Hello," you say, extending your free hand. "I'm impressed by your shop and I'm delighted to meet you."

She can't help but smile. You have done nothing but compliment her.

Get to the point quickly, but don't rush so that you become tongue-tied. Take a deep breath. Pretend to yourself you are selling someone else's work. If she doesn't like yours, it's not your fault, or hers either. This is the hardest part. Don't take offense.

Say, "The (Jones Interiors of Edinboro) has been purchasing my work for (two years) and I've also sold to decorators in (Atlanta and Louisville)." Say whatever you have done that may impress her. Avoid negatives, and don't try to be modest. While you are talking, open your small portfolio and show her some photos of your work. Eventually, tell her that you have a portfolio of original paintings out in the car. Say, "I'll go out and get them," and *go*, if she doesn't stop you. Don't say, "I'll get them if you'd like to see them." That gives her a chance to tell you she is busy.

Bring in your large case and get out your paintings—five or six will do. Say something to indicate the price of your work. I've found it helpful to play my price off against higher prices in other cities or higher-priced artists. You might say, "As you know, original art can have prices as high as ($ __), but when I'm selling mine, unframed, in quantity, I am willing to sell them for ($ __) per painting. They will be matted and wrapped in vinyl for protection. As far as quantity goes, you can have them in lots of (four)." Don't belabor this. Just get in your tiny sales pitch as fast as you can. Stand back and beam as though you had won a lottery. Let's hope she is intrigued. If she's not pleased, leave as quickly and as gracefully as you can and look for another client. And don't get discouraged.

I've been taking you through a presentation to an interior decorator, but there are other types of businesses that buy original art. For large corporations you should vary your technique. There you should not suggest quantity buying. Instead, say that you would like your paintings in their collections, that you would be happy to sell your work unframed so they can select the frame. Try selling your work to individual collectors, banks, and furniture stores. Let them all know that you are willing to work on commission basis. Slant your presentation for each client's individual needs. Keep records on what they say; if they ask you to come back in one month or six months, *do* it. Write it on your calendar and *don't* forget.

About now, you may realize that it would help to have an agent. Yes, but they are hard to come by. Prospective agents are a dime a dozen, but *good* agents must really know you and your art. To be good they must be almost able to think like you. Even if you find a suitable agent, you will have to offer considerable guidance. It is more desirable to learn to be your own agent. Better yet, involve a spouse or close relative in your work or hire other help to take the pressure off of yourself. I find a secretary very useful and I'm living for the day when I can have one full-time. Perhaps a studio assistant can lighten your work load so that your mind can be freer. I never do anything that does not require my presence, but I've never found a substitute for personal contact with art buyers.

Your Special Image

Image is how others perceive us. However, to be effective at anything, you must first perceive yourself as special. Be aware that there are things about you and your art that are different from anyone else. Learn what they are by listening carefully to what viewers say about your work. Play up your specialty in all your brochures and promotions. Then find out who needs your kind of work and go after them.

The thrust of this book is not to teach you how to be a fine artist. I'm trying to help you make money with your art—enough money to support yourself. When you are famous and no longer have to worry about money, you will not regret your hard work during your years of struggle.

Remain true to yourself, but be as interesting as possible to others. No matter what type of personality you are, there is a way to use it to your advantage. Even if you are painfully shy, you can seem mysterious, and it will be an advantage if played upon in the right light. Professional help in writing your printed pieces is so helpful because another specialist in his trade can be objective and bring out your best qualities.

Build yourself a good image. Show yourself to the best advantage.

CHAPTER FIVE

Outdoor Sales and Local Shows

As I've said, there is a pattern to the way an artist should develop and mature in exhibiting. This is the path I'd suggest:

- Nonjuried local shows such as outdoor sales and mall shows
- Juried shows
- Small one-person shows and/or cooperative gallery shows
- Small galleries
- Big galleries
- Museum one-person shows
- Sales to corporations and commissions

It goes without saying that you must be flexible. This schedule might be changed by good fortune. You may receive commissions much ahead of my scheduling.

Get your exhibiting feet wet through outdoor or mall shows. Business-wise, they're relaxed, and you'll benefit by talking to the public. Art magazines often list exhibit opportunities. Many outdoor shows are nonjuried and you may want to try those first. That way you won't face rejection by a jury along with the rest of any misgivings you may have about showing your work. The first time you show your paintings in public you cannot help but feel naked. Every artist does. It is something you learn to live with. In most nonjuried outdoor shows you will pay a fee for a space. The higher the fee, the more exposure you should expect. Sometimes the fee is charged on a percentage of sales. This is my favorite kind of arrangement.

All shows send out a printed *prospectus* on request. This is your set of instructions and should be considered your bible for that particular event. Don't try to bend the rules. If the committee requires that you arrive between ten and noon, rearrange your life so that you can be there. If the prospectus says space will be given on a first-come basis, arrive at eight for a ten o'clock entry time. Get your parking space and do whatever you can for your comfort beforehand. I have never yet managed to be first at the entry line. Artists experienced in outdoor show-

ing are early birds.

Keep records from year to year on each show in a notebook that is just for this purpose. Keep details about the time you arrived, where you parked, what time you actually finished setting up, when the first browser arrived, what time you made your first sale, and when *anyone* made a first sale. Try to find out how many sales were made and the sizes of the sold paintings. Did abstracts sell more than realism? Write it all down. You'll love yourself next year. Keep a record of expenses, too; operate as a business.

A diary of what happened at an outdoor show, like this one from Aline Barker, is invaluable. It tells you everything from what the weather was like to how many sales were made. You should also keep a list of customers' names, addresses, and purchases.

Organizing Your Display

Once again, organization is your best ally. You will need upright display units and a display bin; the units hold framed paintings and the bin holds unframed works. Both need to be portable. Take a look at what other artists use. Visit a show before you exhibit, making notes on everything the artists do.

The display units can be built from conduit and wire mesh. A good design is an A-frame type: two squares of conduit formed into frames covered with wire mesh, then hinged together at the top with wire. The frames should measure about forty inches wide and sixty inches tall, but they can have removable legs so that the frames will fit into a station wagon. Other units are made from peg board or are wooden frames stretched with chicken wire. These constructions can stand up in the manner of room dividers. There are many other ingenious designs you will find used by artists in outdoor shows.

You should have a bin for your unframed work. A good type is a folding container that folds to fit in your car or van, and opens to hold fifty or so sketches.

Cover your sketches with acetate or, better yet, clear vinyl you can buy by the yard. Your work will be well-protected from the elements this way. People can handle the sketches without ruining hundreds of dollars' worth of your work with fingerprints. I mount my sketches on heavy mounting board or museum board. On the back of the sketch, I lay a double thickness of brown paper. Then I cut a piece of vinyl about six inches larger than the sketch. Fold it around the painting, and tape it to the paper. This saves money and provides protection from moisture. If you run into a really rainy day you may wish you had wrapped the whole picture in vinyl and spent a little more money.

PVC pipe makes a great display bin with a Plexiglas bottom. Removing the four screws holding the Plexiglas bottom in place allows the

You don't have to spend a lot of money for display bins. My husband made one of PVC pipe with a Plexiglas bottom. I can remove four screws to release the bottom and knock down the bin to fit in the car. Aline Barker uses two mesh tables, one stacked upside down on the other, with a canvas sling to hold the paintings.

whole bin to come apart and store neatly. One artist who's been successful at outdoor shows, Aline Barker, uses what she calls a "cheapie-quickie" display bin. She adapted little mesh tables to replace her old, very heavy wooden bin. She stacks one on top of the other as shown and secures them with white shoe strings. The hanging slings were made by a friend from white plastic pipe fittings with a canvas drape. The drapes enhance the look, but the little table bins also work well without them. Barker has two of these neat bins and each one holds about twenty-five matted pieces.

There are also *price tags* and *sales records* to consider. Price tags can be stickers you find in office supply stores. It's best to clearly mark a price and not to negotiate each one. I know it's tempting to just let people make offers or try to juggle your prices to suit the clientele, but don't. Base your price on facts. How much do you realistically need to get from the pieces? After you have decided that and marked the paintings plainly, you can quietly come down on a price if a customer asks, and you are willing.

Keep part of your show record notebook for a record of sales. Record the sale, the price, the title and size of the painting, the time of day it sold, and the *name and address of the buyer*. These records are priceless. You will be able to discern patterns of buying habits that will help you to analyze sales. You need the name and address of the buyer for mailings about your next showings.

Here is a checklist of the things needed for an outdoor show:
- Notebook (for records)
- Display unit
- Display bin for matted, unframed pieces
- Vinyl for covering paintings
- Tarpaulin
- Large plastic garbage bags
- Dowels for browse bin
- Rain slicker
- Price stickers
- Indelible ink pen
- Folding lawn chairs
- Food, refreshments
- Ice chest
- Picture wire
- Masking tape
- Drapery hooks to hang paintings on display unit
- Large pieces of cardboard to slip between paintings while carrying
- An assistant to man your booth while you take breaks

Setting Up

Aline Barker is an expert on setting up display space and making it as attractive and comfortable as possible. She begins by organizing her equipment and making it easy to carry. For instance, she had special zippered canvas bags made to order to carry the poles that support her canopy. (Ask at an upholstery or sail-making company to find out who makes custom bags.)

She also pays attention to the distressful dichotomy that comes with outdoor exhibiting: you need good sunny weather to bring out the crowd, but the bright sunlight can damage paintings and the heat can wilt artists. Barker's solution is a 10 x 10-foot canvas canopy. Framed paintings are hung beneath the canopy on folding display racks made from hardware cloth and metal conduit, with unframed paintings in display bins nearby.

Barker also places a table and chairs out *in front* of her display, making it easy for buyers to carry out their transactions. The table's long cloth hides her cooler and tool box—a good idea since junk sitting around is distracting.

With all this done, Barker doesn't hide behind her setup. She stays out where she can make sales and friends. (For more hints from Barker, see the interview on page 52.)

Photos by Clyde Shaw, Louisville, Kentucky

An attractive display is important at any show. Aline Barker starts by assembling the structure that will support her 10 x 10-foot canvas roof, which protects her display from sun or rain, then sets up display racks made from hardware cloth and metal conduit. When she's done, the setting is complete with framed artwork hanging and unframed works in display racks.

Aline Barker
Artist
Louisville, Kentucky

Aline Barker's middle name is organization—no wonder she is dynamic in outdoor shows. She plans everything out very carefully, from what to take along to how to pack the van: "I put things in the van so that the last piece in is what I need first—canopy, then screens, then tool box, etc. Paintings are first in, last out so they can be taken directly to hanging spots and not have to sit on the ground." For more hints on how to handle an outdoor show, read on.

Q. *Aline, where did you get that wonderful equipment for outdoor shows? Did you design all those folding screens, etc.?*

A. I bought the canopy from a company that sells various types of canopies and banners. Art supply stores or display companies should be able to find the type you need.

I designed the screens to fit my van. They are 6 feet tall and 42 inches wide. Two sections are hinged together and have braces to secure a 90-degree angle. I like to set the screens up in a diagonal cross so that customers can walk around and all sides are utilized, giving me eight hanging spaces plus good viewing advantage for each space. The screens were made of hardware cloth and conduit.

Q. *How difficult is it to set up your area? Could you do it by yourself if necessary?*

A. With two people, set-up is a breeze. I do not think I could do it alone on concrete, but on grass, where I could drive a stake in the ground to stabilize one end, I think I could manage by using an extra half hour of set-up time. I do not want help in hanging the paintings. Those placement decisions I want to make by myself so that I am satisfied with the total exhibit.

Q. *How long does it take to set up?*

A. I allow one hour overall. This allows me time to make a nice arrangement of paintings. This is minimum. Since I do not like to rush, I try to arrive early. Two people can actually have the canopy set up in ten minutes, but I don't like to be in such a hurry that I can't have a cup of coffee with a neighbor.

Q. *How many shows per year do you think it is feasible for an artist to attempt?*

A. At my age, a total of six shows is a lot for me. However, I know a number of younger artists who do as many as twenty per year. I think this is an individual choice. Some people like this way of life so much that they go out week after week.

Q. *How do you find shows?*

A. I know and am very selective of our regional shows. Others, such as the Cobb County Show, near Atlanta, I attend on the recommendation of other artists.

Q. *What is your criteria for a suitable show?*

A. A record of *good sales* and *publicity*. *Attractive grounds* that lend themselves to attractive set-ups. Park-like exhibit spaces draw people. *Accessibility.* Can I pull the van up into the space? A *host group that cares* about the artists and provides adequate parking and rest-room facilities, etc.

Q. *Do you keep records on shows from year to year? What kind of information is important?*

A. I keep a notebook on my table and ask buyers to write their name and address while I am getting their purchases ready. I always list the dollar amount of the sale and some descriptive info. I use this procedure for sales from my studio or anywhere—not just at outdoor shows. I use this list when making out invitations to my one-person shows. In my outdoor show book, I reserve a page for each show to record what time of the day peak sales happened and what the weather was like.

Q. *What advice would you have for artists wanting to get into and sell at outdoor shows?*

A. Before you begin to exhibit, attend a number of outdoor shows, and:

• Note the set-ups.

• Consider which shows would be most suitable to your work. If some artists are not involved with a customer, discuss the show with them.

• Especially notice work similar to yours. Is it getting the attention of the buyers?

• Study the price ranges. Are prices realistic? Are people buying?

• Recognize that an established artist will be able to charge more than a newcomer.

• Be as observant as possible.

• Learn from others' experience.

Surviving the Elements

On the show circuit, rain is something you must contend with—and sometimes you do contend! It's best to prepare for that possibility right from the start. Rain clouds have been known to travel hundreds of miles out of their way just to attend an outdoor art exhibit. Always carry a tarpaulin with you to your booth. Have some plastic garbage bags on hand; you can stick all of your paintings and paraphernalia into them in an emergency.

Set up your display in such a way that you can get the paintings off the panels and into bags quickly. Paintings can survive rain pretty well in bags leaning upright against the bin under the tarp. Have a rain drill—the way you used to have a fire drill in school. Plan the quickest way to get your work to your car. Have your browse bin built so that there is an opening in the bottom to let rain water drain out. Keep a rain slicker with your show equipment. Who knows? It may keep the rain away.

Wooden dowels about a half an inch in diameter and about the width of your bin should be kept in the bottom of your browse bin. When it's time to stack your paintings, lay the dowels down first and stack the painting across them. This keeps the artwork away from the wet ground.

When marking the price tags, think again of rain and moisture. Use waterproof ink.

Most problems of outdoor exhibiting can be anticipated and solved before they happen. We've talked about rain, but there is also sun—almost equally as devastating to paintings and to you. Find an exhibit space in the shade if you can. Rig some kind of sun shade without destroying the visibility of the paintings. Take folding lawn chairs with you, and find a way to attach sun umbrellas to them. Beach equipment sometimes works well. One year I took my large picnic table umbrella and set it up in such a way as to shade the whole display. It worked surprisingly well and we moved it several times during the day.

Kathryn Witte
Artist
Louisville, Kentucky

Kathryn Witte is an artist who enjoys every facet of her artistic life and always has. Sorry if she sounds too good to be true, but over all the years I've known her, I've never heard her complain when her work was not selling or about the rain at outdoor shows or the price of pigment these days. I've heard her mention those things, but always with a twinkle in her eye. She honestly seems to feel that everything that comes her way is a blessing, either outright or in disguise, and it shows in her joyous paintings and her popularity in the Louisville art scene. Her work can be seen at the J. B. Speed Museum Gallery and several other galleries in Kentucky and Indiana plus most of the good outdoor shows within comfortable traveling distance of her home.

Q. *You are a successful art fair exhibitor. I know that you choose to be selective regarding your shows and to live a slow-paced life. Still, you are successful and probably could make any amount of money you desire. Would you share your thoughts on art fairs with us?*

A. Don't belittle the importance of art fairs for making money as an artist. Fairs are a way of making quick cash sales as well as good contacts for future sales. Remember, this is a fun venture to be enjoyed with the public. Be well organized before the opening day. Keep everything as simple as possible. Paintings should be matted, covered with acetate, and priced. Personally, I take only work that I am proud of—not the failures to sell cheap.

Since I have no help in setting up my booth, I make it easy for me. My bin (homemade) folds up and fits in my car trunk. I use two or three pegboards (A-line) for display. I always take two folding chairs—one is for the tired visitor. That chair always faces my paintings and usually the visit ends in a purchase.

Q. *How many paintings do you take to a show?*

A. I think too many pictures in a booth boggles the mind of the buyer. Be selective. Display only a few of your best at a time. As you sell, put others out.

Q. *What is your best hint for success to beginning fair exhibitors?*

A. Enjoy yourself! I think this is one of the secrets of a successful venture. Talk, laugh, and kid with the people. People come to the fairs to be entertained as well as to buy. Time your talking with them to be after they have shown sufficient interest in your work. You soon learn that every person who passes your booth is not a prospective buyer. Beware of looking bored or reading a book. And remember to stay until the closing hour; many sales are made then.

An ice chest is another comfort must.

Exhibiting in an outdoor or mall show can be an enjoyable experience. You must go armed with a sense of humor. Listening to the public's comments is a unique experience. The different attitudes that people have about artists have always intrigued me. I once listened while someone who was familiar with my work, but who did not know me by sight, explained why I was in my *Onion Period. I* didn't even know I was in an *Onion Period*. I just didn't have the courage to tell the viewer that he was talking to the artist; I was too fascinated to hear his views to stop him. Then, after he'd gone so far, I couldn't think of a way to tell him without bursting into laughter. I spent the rest of the show furtively glancing around to make sure he did not come upon me unawares and find out who I really was.

Painting for the Crowd

Many artists demonstrate their painting techniques at their booths. I don't do much of this anymore, but I do sketch a lot. When an artist is sitting and sketching with pen and pad, people always come up to look and good conversations begin. In fact, my favorite trick in getting to know people anywhere is to take a small sketch book and sit on a wall at an outdoor concert, or lean against my car on some historic street, and sketch. People stop, look through the book and say, "What would you charge for a painting done from this sketch?" I've sold many a commission from my sketch book. I've even sketched at parties. I'm not an exhibitionist and I never do it when I feel the occasion is too formal. But, I feel whole with a pencil or pen in my hand. I feel at ease and that puts others at ease. If you demonstrate at shows, be prepared to be interrupted. Do something that is easy and fun for you; don't tackle a masterpiece.

Outdoor and mall shows are the best way in the world to pay your dues as an artist. They prepare you for better things to come, and from them you will learn things about handling yourself as an artist that you can't learn anywhere else. Some artists find outdoor or mall shows to be their main source for sales.

Juried Art Exhibitions

When are you ready to enter a juried show? That is an exhibit that has a judge or jury to accept or reject your painting and to give awards. Jury information plus all the other regulations are always printed in a brochure about the show called a *prospectus*. You are ready to enter these shows as soon as you are ready to find out what the rest of the art world thinks of your work.

To find juried shows, watch your newspaper for local opportunities and read the art magazines for shows in the rest of the country.

First, send for the prospectus. Deadlines for entering are sometimes months ahead of show time, so be prepared to think far in advance. When you get the prospectus, read it carefully and do whatever it requires for entry. Usually the prospectus will ask you to submit color transparencies of your work. Read the eligibility section, so you won't enter acrylic-coated caseins in a watercolor show demanding work on paper and unvarnished. Select your best work by the photographic slide, not by the original, since the jury will see only the slide. Pay attention to the size limitations listed on the prospectus and stick to the framing regulations. Fill out the entry blank that comes with the prospectus.

Paying attention to detail will not ensure your acceptance into the show. Nothing can do that, but you can save yourself a lot of grief by being meticulous. Prove you are a pro even if it is your first experience. Your first show can be traumatic. Whatever happens to you, be it good or bad, will probably be reversed in your second show or soon thereafter. Be prepared for many ups and downs; they will continue as long as you are exhibiting.

Understanding the System

Find out how shows work by volunteering to help. Work on as many exhibit committees as you can. You will soon see that the problems involved in selecting work and hanging shows make it almost impossible to be fair. In this case, it's better to try to think negatively for a change.

Don't expect to get into shows. Don't hope to win awards. Consider it all a learning experience, or somewhat like gambling. Then when a good thing comes along, it will be wonderful.

If you are rejected, remember that your rejection comes from the personality of the juror, not necessarily from the quality of your work. When there is exhibit space for sixty paintings and the show committee finds three hundred entries on their hands, you know that some very good work has to lose out. What would you do, if you were the juror, after you have "thrown out" all the work that you feel is weak and you still have two hundred good paintings facing you with only sixty spaces available? As a juror, you may be tempted to flip a coin. Even then, the first time around, you'll only get rid of 50 percent of the paintings, and you still have to eliminate forty more in some way. The problems faced by exhibit committees and jurors are monumental.

Back when I entered almost every show that came along, I used to keep a record of what happened to my work under each juror. Then, when I faced that juror again, I'd know what he liked or did not like when he last saw my work. No one gives you a report on what happened to your work. No one can possibly tell you why the juror did not select your offering. You have to figure out these things for yourself from whatever pattern you discern. If you work on the show committee, you have a chance of overhearing things that will help you make decisions about your work. But, even when you do hear something a juror says about your work, you have not exactly heard the word of God; the next juror may feel differently. After a while, you begin to take it all with a grain of salt and come to realize that you only compete with yourself.

Don't give up on entering the shows. It is one of the best ways to grow as an artist. When you are successful in one area, move up to more prestigious shows with better artists. The day will come when you no longer have time to enter every show. Later, when you are well known, you may have no time for shows at all. But if you haven't taken your knocks in exhibits, and paid your dues, how will you ever let the world know you exist?

Completing the Picture

There are some extra things you can do, besides creating good art, that will help your chances in a show. One is good framing. I've heard juror after juror complain about the bad frames many artists use. A frame is an integral part of the painting. The nicest frame I ever saw was on a John Marin painting that still hangs over the fireplace in the room in his studio-home at Cape Split, Maine, where he died. He made the frame at the same time he created the painting. It is roughhewn and covered with the same paint as the painting. It is such a work of art that I felt I was looking at a painting that turned into sculpture at the frame's edge. A frame should always be subordinate to the painting and never overpower it. You cannot always trust a framer to do it right. You must tell her exactly what you want. It's up to you to choose the frame and the mat color.

Slides, Shipping, and Fees

Today, jurors only look at slides to judge most shows. There are ways you can help yourself when faced with slide jurying. Be sure the slide is clear and sharp and has enough contrast to *grab* the eye. Photograph the painting *straight on*, so it is square on the slide. Don't include the frame in the picture. If any background shows on the transparency, block it out with silver tape that you can buy in photography shops. (See Keets Rivers' example of a bad slide at right.) Follow religiously the prospectus directions for labeling.

When choosing the slides to enter, I check mine against good slides of other artists' paintings. I acquire as many slides of the work of artist

friends as I can—artists who are frequently successful in shows. If my slide holds up well against theirs, it has a better chance to hold up against other good artists in the next show.

Shipping the accepted pictures to shows can be a headache. Check out United Parcel Service (UPS), air freight, and Greyhound to find out the size limit on shipments. When you send a painting by UPS or some other shipping service, they will ask you what is inside. Tell them it is artwork, without glass, and is replaceable by money. That is an answer that meets all of their

"Echoing Arches," Keets Rivers, 22 x 28 inches, acrylic.

This is an example of how *not* to position a painting for an entry in a professional exhibit. All the extra space and mat should be blocked out.

requirements except size. You may need to have a crate to assure safe handling. Sometimes you can get mirror boxes from furniture stores that are a big help. Some artists solve shipping problems by helping one another. They ship paintings to each other unframed and take them to framers in their own towns for each other. Vanning art is also becoming popular. If you belong to an art group with several artists who are sending paintings to the same show, think of joining together to hire a van and driver.

How about the fees for juried shows? They are necessary to pay the jurors and exhibit space rent, plus other show expenses, and are not refundable. When your work is not accepted in a show, consider the fee as your contribution to the welfare of the art world.

Checklist for exhibiting in juried shows:
- Send for prospectus of as many shows as you can
- Return entry blanks, slides, and fees *on time*
- Mark dates of shipping, jurying, returns, etc.
- Use proper framing (sturdy for shipping but not heavy or overpowering)
- Send good color slides of your artwork
- Pack the art in shipping crates (made with strong sides)
- Use Plexiglas on paintings instead of glass

Entering a juried show can be the most challenging and the most frightening step you take in your career. Your first show will be remembered all your life after others have blurred. It's hard. The best way to go at it is not to think about it. Enter shows as though you were performing a ritual. At least you won't be executed if you're not accepted. Don't consider rejection as failure; consider the whole thing an experiment. It's a lot like horse racing—get yourself to the starting gate.

Keets Rivers, an experienced show handler, lists reasons why a painting might be accepted or rejected during the jurying process.

Keets Rivers
Painter, Sculptor
Pensacola, Florida

Painter and sculptor Keets Rivers has extensive experience in jurying exhibits and in selecting and working with jurors for exhibits in many areas of the country. For ten years she wrote a monthly column about art shows for Sunshine Artists U.S.A. She also taught painting for many years and was one of the group of seven or so energetic artists who started Pensacola Artists Inc., a co-op art gallery.

Q. *What do you think judges look for in a painting when jurying an art show?*
A. Strength in composition and in value patterns and possibly a new approach to creativity.

Q. *What do you think would be a judge's most frequent reason for accepting a painting for exhibit?*
A. A well-rounded, full statement in the work of art with visual impact, be it mood, character, value, or outstanding execution.

Q. *What most often causes an artist's painting to be rejected?*

A. A painting that has many hours of "loving hands" work but just not the right experience or expertise. Often these same artists will apply for another exhibit at a later date and do very well. That is why it is so important to try again and continue on the stepping stones to success.

Q. *How early in a career should an artist begin to enter exhibits?*

A. When the artist feels he or she may be ready. Not when family and friends all want a painting. Artist friends may be helpful in starting a new artist out but not always truthful. Start with small local outdoor shows or smaller gallery shows. If you are well received by the viewing and buying public, then try a larger exhibit in the area. In addition to the needed exposure, you will also benefit from seeing your artwork beside the work of other artists. "Things" will show up that went unnoticed in the studio. Being out in the big wide world does make a difference.

Q. *Do you think jurors rely on their personal taste to judge work?*

A. It has some bearing, of course. But all knowledgeable jurors will consider points of composition, value, color quality, center of interest, depth of vision, mood or character, execution, and impact. Personal preferences can't be ignored, but basic points should always be considered.

Q. *Could you be more specific about those points that jurors should consider?*

A. Of course.

Composition — how you arrange the elements of design on your painting.

Value — the relationship and placement of light and dark elements in a painting.

Color quality — the warm or cool characteristics, the hue or intensity of color in a painting.

Center of interest — to be found by directional or action lines and value relationships.

Depth of vision — for realistic painting: foreground, middle ground, distance. For abstract painting: overlapping planes.

Execution — the brushstrokes or washes well done. Or the painting carried to completion competently.

Mood or character — the feeling or movement. The tension or attraction to you. What is the impact? Will this painting stop you when viewed from across the room?

Q. *What parting words do you have for artists who want to enter juried shows?*

A. Try to set some goals along the way — short term and long term. Remember they can always be changed or discarded. Just knowing what you are aiming for in a given time will help you attain some of the goals.

Your love of art is a very demanding and time-consuming thing. Try not to expect it all to "jell" overnight.

CHAPTER SEVEN

Galleries and Museums

There are as many kinds of galleries as there are artists. There are commercial galleries and sophisticated galleries, each with its own clientele and price range. Some galleries are in business to make money, some are tax write-offs. Your challenge is to find one that will benefit *you*, regardless of the gallery's motives.

You will probably start exhibiting in one of the less sophisticated galleries and then move on to better ones. It is best to start in one small town and then graduate to bigger galleries in larger towns until you are exhibiting where you want to be—New York, Chicago, San Francisco, Washington, D.C. That way no hard feelings are created by changing galleries in the same town.

You can wait to be discovered in a local exhibit or you can build up a portfolio to make a presentation, such as I described earlier. The latter is the better approach. Don't wait to have good things happen. Instead, *make* things happen. Start by phoning some of the galleries in your area. Ask whether they are accepting new artists. Tell them what they need to know about you. Find out what kind of art they like, but *never change your style for a gallery*. You can be influenced by what others think, but when you change your style of painting, it should be because of some natural growth coming from within yourself. I've stressed this before, but I can't say it enough. Whenever you seek others' opinions, always weigh their advice against your own thoughts. Keep yourself open and in a growth process. This is particularly important in dealing with a gallery. Try to find a gallery that fits your own style.

Going to the galleries in person is sometimes better than phoning. You can walk in and browse without even suggesting you are an artist. See if your work belongs there. Perhaps you will feel so good about the place that you will want to introduce yourself before you leave and make an appointment to show your work to the director.

Be prepared for surprises when you make your presentation. Sometimes there's a great rapport from the start, but even now, with my work in several galleries and museums, I sometimes encounter a negative response from a new gallery. It's a puzzling experience. Sometimes the rejection is simply because the gallery already has an artist whose technique is very much like yours. For instance, one director had told me that my work did not appeal to his clientele. Strange—I had looked at the paintings on his gallery's walls and felt that several of the works were close to my kind of painting, but I didn't argue with him. I liked this gallery enough that I asked for a chance to show him some other types of artwork. He agreed. However, it is best not to try to beat a dead horse. If you encounter this situation, you can decide whether to go back but you *must* go on to seek other galleries. For every artist, there is a gallery, many galleries, that will be glad to try to sell that artist's work.

Cooperative Galleries

Cooperative galleries are a comfortable way for an artist to enter the exhibiting arena. Many cities have art centers run by artists. In my formative years, I was accepted by the Arts and Crafts Center of Pittsburgh—a very professional group—and it was extremely good for my career. An artist must first be professionally screened by her peers to be accepted by one of the member groups, such as Associated Artists of Pittsburgh or the Society of Sculptors. After that, an artist has the right to exhibit in the galleries and teach at the teaching center, and must work for the organization. Members are expected to put in time selling and cleaning, and to handle all the chores connected with an art center.

In Washington, D.C., there is an interesting group of artists in the Torpedo Factory Art Center. The Torpedo Factory is run in a way different from the Pittsburgh group. After being accepted, an artist rents studio space and works there a certain number of hours each week. The artist exhibits from his own studio.

In Chicago there is a group called the American Society of Artists, another kind of cooperative that accepts members from all over the country. They run a cooperative gallery by paying people to sell the work, list their artists on a lecture service, and send out mailings about their activities on request.

Make a few inquiries in your area and you will find your niche. There are smaller, less formidable cooperatives, too. Many small art centers accept artists without any screening of their work. Try those first; then move on.

Gallery Sales

Gallery selling will probably contribute to part of your income, but some artists sell only through galleries and have their commissions handled only through them. If you plan to sell through galleries exclusively, you may want to be represented by several galleries. You *can* have more than one gallery, but no more than one per small town. In large urban areas you might have several galleries; one, say, in Bethesda, Maryland, and another in Alexandria, Virginia, both of which would be in the Washington, D.C. area, but widely separated. It depends on the requirements of your galleries. Some galleries consider a certain number of miles to be their area and request you to be exclusive with them in that area. Be sure you want to give them their demands before you join a gallery. Get a contract that spells everything out. Galleries usually provide these. (See Chapter 9 for information on how to protect your work, gallery bankruptcy, and copyright.)

Locating Galleries

When you feel it is time for you to exhibit out of town, how do you find a gallery? Write to them, of course. Buy copies of art magazines—the kind read by collectors as well as artists. Look at the gallery ads and review them for six months or so to find some that look as though your work would

Marge Alderson
Former President
The Torpedo Factory Art Center
Alexandria, Virginia

Since the Torpedo Factory Art Center began in 1974, Marge Alderson has been part of the cooperative. She served as president, was an original board member, and also has had a studio there. Here she tells the advantages of cooperatives, how they work, and how to join one.

Q. *You were the director of an artist's cooperative for about seven years and are an artist also. You must be well informed about what the world wants from an artist.*

A. Yes, I'm a watercolorist; and yes, I have always spent a lot of time concerned with art professionalism.

Q. *Why would collective studio space be advantageous to an artist?*

A. For the cost of rental space in our center, the artist achieves these goals: a place to work; a place to sell; a place to interact with

63

other artists; a place to compete and exhibit; and, a place to teach and study since there is an art school here.

All this, plus the fact that this center is publicly owned and provides reasonable rental space, makes this an attractive alternative to private studio space.

Q. *How does an artist go about acquiring space here?*

A. You apply by coming in and inquiring. An artist will be asked to submit work to a panel of three judges—top professionals who are not connected with the center. Judges are selected through recommendations of members of the center, who suggest the names of top people in their fields. The jury is directed to choose artists with work comparable to, or better than, art already in the center. Our jury is made up of artists knowledgeable in three-dimensional work, two-dimensional work, and fine crafts. Screening takes place two times a year.

Q. *What is the biggest stumbling block for an artist facing the jury?*

A. Presentation. Poor or inappropriate matting, i.e., colored mats, sloppy framing (matting and framing are not taut enough). But there are places an artist can learn. I've discovered that frame-it-yourself places do teach this and have a lot of good information, but they are not slanted toward the prejudices of jurors in the art world. An artist should show his pride in his work by the way he presents it. The work itself should be consistent in technique, approach, and quality. This is definitely not the time to show a retrospective of your work for the past twenty years! It should be current work and it shouldn't say, I just tossed this off. It should be professional.

Q. *Please define the word professional, as a juror would.*

A. For passing a jury, more than anything else, it's attitude—an attitude that denotes experience. The way an artist presents his work reflects knowledge of accepted standards and disciplined personal direction toward improvement.

Q. *To be a professional artist you need to do more than pass a jury from time to time, wouldn't you say?*

A. Yes, and believe it or not, the Internal Revenue Service (IRS) provides a good guideline as to what a professional artist must do. If an artist is not doing those things, he's probably not yet a pro. Contact your IRS office to see what guidelines might be available for you as a professional artist.

fit. Send letters and your biography, any good printed pieces about you, and slides of at least five paintings. Some galleries want a long track record, so don't be modest.

Be prepared to write many letters and to spend a good deal of time on this. Eventually, you may have enough responses to merit a trip to the new city to check out the galleries in person. More likely you will end up just sending work. In that case, be sure to send your work in such a way that you receive a signature of acceptance from someone at the gallery. Know where your paintings are at all times.

At the time this book was written, most galleries charged at least a 40 percent commission. Some galleries have gone as high as 60 percent. They do have a problem of survival, but the artist also suffers in giving up all that money, especially when the artist bears all the cost of framing and shipping. A good gallery will make contacts for the artist, have a one-person show at least every one or two years, pay at least half of the artist's reception costs, and sell at least one painting per month. Sales galleries in smaller museums sometimes take only 20 percent commission. Many of the cooperative galleries also have low commission rates. Cooperative galleries may split expenses in a different way than commercial galleries. Sometimes it is hard for us not to feel that everyone is making money from our efforts. Try to grin and bear it. We need galleries, and until someone comes up with a better way to sell art, we must pay the price.

I have found a few of the smaller galleries will buy my work outright. That helps because I don't have the suspense of waiting for a painting to sell. When you find a gallery that will do this, go for it! If your work sells higher than you expected, just charge more the next time. Be delighted it went that way, instead of the gallery being stuck with your unwanted work.

How does a gallery find an artist it wants to exhibit and what are some of the problems a gallery faces? Read the interview with Katharine Amsler for information from a gallery owner's point of view.

Each gallery director is different and not all have time to be kind. One gallery director in a very large city told me that she never wants in-person calls from an artist until that artist has sent her three to five slides with a stamped, self-addressed envelope and a phone number but no résumé. She doesn't have enough time to read résumés. She just wants to see the work and then will notify the artist if she wants to see more. She says that at times she may be as much as five months behind in her answers to artists—and it bothers her greatly. Extreme patience from the artist is required but she is doing the best she can. Of course she is in a very busy metropolitan area. So each gallery is different and you must feel your way.

Presenting Your Work

After you have found a gallery of your choice, phone to make the appointment. Before your meeting, reorganize your portfolio of photos of paintings to gear it to this specific presentation. Take out any photos you think will not appeal to this particular gallery. Run through an imaginary presentation in your mind. Be prepared to answer all questions, preferably with some photos or printed material about yourself.

Use your small portfolio. Include photos of all of your paintings that fit the image of the gallery you are approaching. Take slides of other good works and your small viewer to show the slides properly. Be sure to have your printed résumé and a longer biography showing everything that you have done. Be prompt and organized. Keep your things conveniently packed so that you can find them quickly, making the presentation go smoothly.

Use psychology on yourself and the gallery director. Keep in mind how good you are—if there is interest in your work, your confidence will further impress the director. Don't rush, but don't waste the director's time. Take his lead. If he seems chatty, chat; but if he seems harried, get to the point. Be flexible. If some unforeseen emergency has entered his day, you might suggest that, if he wishes, you can come back. Of course, you mind doing this—but try to act as if his welfare comes first. It may swing the pendulum in your favor.

However, if the director seems disinterested in your work, then the gallery is probably not for you. It's hard to accept rejection kindly, but try. Getting upset or arguing with a gallery director only hurts you. Never try to justify or defend your work. Be positive. If it's no go, head for the next gallery. Rejections of an artist's work are not rejections of the artist, so don't take them personally. Keep in mind the good things that have happened to you.

When considering a gallery presentation, review Chapter 4.

Recording Consignments

If your work is accepted by a gallery, the gallery will probably have a contract for you to sign. Review it carefully, noting the elements mentioned in Chapter 10. You may also want to keep your own consignment records. They can be made up on memos that you can buy in office supply stores. An example:

This is to certify that on _____(date)_____ I left on consignment with _____(gallery name)_____, _____(number)_____ paintings to be sold with a _____(amount)_____ percent commission of the retail price to be retained by the gallery.

List the title, medium, size, whether framed or unframed, and retail price for each painting. For example:

1. Fall Roses, watercolor, 22 x 30 inches framed; retail price $400.
2. Midnight Sun, acrylic on canvas, 24 x 44

inches framed; retail price $1,200.
3. Driftwood Bay, watercolor, 22 x 30 inches unframed; retail price $250.

Artist (signature) _____
Gallery Director (signature) _____
Address of gallery _____
Phone number of gallery _____

You can type these up a few at a time to save printing costs or they can be handwritten. Don't leave paintings without records. If you choose to use only the gallery's forms, that's okay. Don't forget, in your excitement about having your work shown, to get a *signature* on a receipt.

Buy a special notebook for recording sales and keeping other records on galleries. Paste your consignment slips in this book. Your sales slips go into your tax record book. Keep a record of sales in both the gallery notebook and the tax record book. (You will find more about taxes in Chapter 10.)

Gallery Checklist

Now that you are showing in galleries, review all the criteria for being professional. Be sure your framing is attractive and sturdy. Never take a painting out of a gallery in order to sell it to a client at a lower price, even if some buyers suggest it to you. This is one reason that galleries like to sell work from artists who live out of town. Be careful to keep your prices fairly consistent all across the country. If you sell in Chicago and also in Pittsburgh, or even in such widely separated cities as San Francisco and New York, you will be surprised at how often a person from one area will see your work in another. If they see it at a cheaper price than the one they paid, you may be in for trouble. It is important to figure your prices by some realistic method. Charge what you honestly feel the traffic will bear for your work, and stick to it. Go up gradually.

Checklist for exhibiting in galleries:

Charles Pitcher
Artist
Pittsburgh, Pennsylvania

Pitcher's intimate and sensitive landscapes, painted in oil or transparent watercolor, have won many awards. His work is in the homes of over five hundred private collectors and is included in many corporate collections.

Q. *What kind of gallery connections do you have?*

A. Right now, I'm under contract to one gallery in my home area. But I have two others in more distant towns.

Q. *How many galleries do you think an artist should have to produce a decent income?*

A. For me, it takes about three which are really working for me. If I get involved with a couple that do not sell as fast, then I would need about five galleries. In other words, three hard-working galleries or five slow-moving galleries. Each gallery should sell one painting per month on the average. I once went seven months without any income, but the galleries had all sold about double their average right before that. Then sales picked up again and

I was back on an even keel. But those seven months were very hard to take. When something like that happens, you wonder if you will ever make a sale again. Generally, the gallery sales average has stayed constant. An artist has to learn to live with things like that. It's frightening, but you have to keep the faith.

I keep about six paintings in each gallery at all times. In the out-of-town galleries, I change unsold paintings once a year. At home, I change two or three paintings every six weeks or so. Nothing is ever left for more than a year. Even that may be too long. It's a good idea to remove paintings often, so your public gets to know that they do not have forever to make up their minds to buy.

Q. *Your galleries are all commercial, aren't they? Do you ever sell in cooperative space?*

A. I used to sell in co-ops. They are cheaper. The commission is lower, but I feel that the people who run them don't always have the drive of the commerical galleries. Don't get me wrong, I'm not putting the co-ops down, but the gallery owner who knows he has to live by selling has more incentive. No matter how much effort the co-op people put in, they know they won't starve if they don't sell. Of course, if it's artists who are running the co-op, sometimes you get into other problems. I feel commercial galleries have produced better for me.

Q. *What advice do you have for artists just starting out?*

A. Establish a reputation in your own back yard. Professional shows, professional organizations, awards—do as much as you can. Get your name before the public. The people who buy art only know what they hear, see, or read. That's all. Visibility—that's the key. And take heart; it does work.

Katharine Amsler
Owner/Director
Bird in the Hand Gallery
Sewickley, Pennsylvania

A gallery director has to be an artist, in a way, too. An artist at creating an atmosphere conducive to selling art. As a gallery director for almost twenty years, Katharine Amsler has a few tips for artists seeking new galleries.

Q. *Katharine, how do you find your exhibiting artists?*

A. I have now had a gallery for going on twenty years so here I seem to have no problem. They find me, although I still go to art shows all over the country and also sometimes out of the country (I just had a successful show from Peru). I am always looking for new talent—something different.

Q. *If the artist is seeking you out, how do you like an artist to present work?*

A. I like to see slides—although I also like to see a few pieces of the actual work. Sometimes the slides don't really tell the whole story. I am a stickler for presentation—good matting, good framing, etc.

Q. *What is good matting and good framing?*

A. For a show in the gallery, I usually prefer strip framing with mitered corners or the simple metal framing. The show "hangs together" better than if frames are all different kinds of molding. Mats can be either single, double, or triple but must have clean cut *beveled* edges.

Q. *How do you feel outdoor shows in your area affect gallery sales?*

A. They don't affect my gallery. In fact, there is a big outdoor show every year right in front of the Bird in the Hand. If anything, that show brings new people in. I like the street trade. A lot of the gallery artists do not take part in outdoor shows.

Q. *How does the general art picture look to you?*

A. Well—I'm still here—in spite of the bad times in Pittsburgh. It (the sales) did fall off a bit for a while, but people who like and want good pieces of artwork still seem to buy and I see nothing wrong with layaway, especially for the younger buyers.

Q. *What suggestions would you give to artists just beginning to show?*

A. The thing I stress the most is presentation. This, to me, makes all the difference. Of course, I have to like the work, and I sell all kinds—abstract, impressionism, realism.

The manner of the artist also counts. Be sure of yourself but not pushy! And, of course, a well-organized portfolio of work is a must! By an organized portfolio, I mean a good presentation of an artist's work: not too many pieces or it gets boring, just what the artist feels to be the best pieces he/she has to offer. Again, neat. The work should be shrink-packed if not framed.

- Art magazines to locate galleries
- Brochure to send to galleries
- Portfolio to show galleries
- Color slides of your work and portable projector
- Plexiglas instead of glass on paintings
- Consignment record for gallery to sign
- Notebook to keep record of sales and consignments

After you become established with a gallery, you should constantly evaluate both your performance and the gallery's. Are they selling for you? If a gallery is not generating at least one sale a month for me, I feel I'm not being properly represented. These sales can be averaged over several months to arrive at a fair number of paintings sold. If, for example, you had a one-person show and sold twelve paintings, then you could say the gallery was producing one sale per month for that year. Remember, if you don't keep the gallery supplied with enough work, you can't expect sales. It works both ways.

Here are some comments from an artist who has tried the New York gallery scene for the past few years:

"It's tough here. It's not the place for beginners or those with low stamina. Art, at best, is hard work and in New York, it is doubly hard. The competition here is so fierce that it's frightening. The galleries are swamped with artists trying to be discovered. Of course, if you are good enough, you will be discovered, but it takes time and tremendous effort."

Museums

Museum exhibiting is usually considered to be the ultimate kind of show—the most prestigious for an artist—and it is not easy to come by. If the chance should come your way early in your career, and you have enough paintings to make a good showing (at least fifty good ones stacked up and waiting for the choosing) take it—don't hesitate a minute. But don't expect a museum show to happen until you are very well established.

If you ever need to make the choice between a show that you know will produce very good sales and a museum show where you aren't sure just how many buyers there will be, I'd advise choosing the museum. Museums look very good on your résumé, providing the kind of high profile that produces commissions and general well-being in the art world far into the future. As it is with anything in your life, it's best not to charge ahead without some research. Find out if the museum of your choice is interested in contemporary artists and what credentials you will need to qualify. Otherwise you could embarrass yourself by asking for pie in the sky.

Millard F. Rogers, Jr.
Director
Cincinnati Art Museum
Cincinnati, Ohio

As director of the Cincinnati Art Museum, Millard F. Rogers, Jr. has his finger on the pulse of the whole art world. Here he tells how museums decide what to display.

Q. *When do artists get the opportunity to exhibit at a museum?*

A. As a preface to my answer I want to say that the thing I find artists fail so often to do is to explore the focus of the particular museum that interests them — is it contemporary or modern or Old Master, or is it a little of everything, as the Cincinnati Art Museum is? My plea to artists is to save a lot of time and grief by exploring the above before writing to any institution to request an exhibition. Also, an artist should explore why he/she wants to exhibit in a museum. For more attention? Notoriety — to add a prestigious institution to the artist's résumé? What purpose will be served for *both* the artist and the museum?

The policy for the Cincinnati Art Museum is that we stage eight to twelve temporary exhibitions per year and they have a wide range, trying to reflect the collecting focus of this museum. The exhibitions are not all by living artists. It takes three to five years to get a show into the exhibition schedule. When the Exhibition Planning Committee meets, proposal forms prepared by the various curators and the director are presented. These proposals may be for rentals from the Smithsonian, or an Old Master show from a museum in Europe, or for exhibitions such as the one we did this year called *Simply Stunning* which depicted the changes in ladies' fashions in the last 200 years. The proposals are very well supported by slides and past history and other proofs that this exhibition will be beneficial to the museum.

Q. *Do you do one-person shows very often?*

A. We don't generally do exhibitions for single artists (that is, one-person shows). We try to stage exhibitions that only our museum can do. Other smaller museums and galleries *can* do one-person contemporary shows but they *can't* do such shows as *Masterworks from Munich* because of a lack of staffing or space requirements or whatever, so we don't step over into their area; we let them do what they can do best and we do what we do best. Occasionally, artists of recognized stature are given shows. Usually these have international reputations. We do not organize or put on exhibitions by regional or local artists except on rare occasions. One of the shows for a single artist that we did have was the Richard Diebenkorn exhibition, as an example.

Q. *How do you keep up with the current art scene?*

A. We are interested in what is coming on in art and we do like to find out what contemporary artists are producing. Periodically, we do an invitational exhibition of area artists. We find these artists through galleries and other artists we already know. This is a group show.

Other museums handle new artists in other ways and each institution is different. Some, like the Cleveland Museum and the Art Museum in Evansville, Indiana, have yearly juried shows for living artists. Juried exhibitions are listed in various art journals and special-interest magazines. Frequently, they are open only to artists from the museum's region.

CHAPTER EIGHT

Alternative Spaces

Exhibiting in galleries and museums isn't the only alternative at this stage of your career. You can also open your own gallery for the exhibit of your work *only* or seek out alternative spaces such as those in libraries or universities.

Opening Your Own Gallery

Opening your own gallery in a place of business, as opposed to Autry Dye's home gallery space on pages 27-29, takes dedication and daring but it proved a very good solution for me.

Right here it should be made clear again that I wholeheartedly approve of commercial galleries. We artists have a great need for them. But in certain situations a one-artist gallery is desirable. When you happen to be well known in your locality—as I have usually been, whether living in a large city like Pittsburgh or a small town, as I now do—clients soon begin to call you instead of your galleries about your work. I have always been scrupulously fair about this. If ever a client saw my work in a gallery and then asked me to withdraw a painting from that gallery and sell it direct (splitting the gallery commission with the client), I always said no, loud and clear. If the client then purchased other paintings directly from me, I would always give the gallery a commission and inform both the client and the gallery just what was happening. The prices in my home studio were always kept consistent with the gallery prices.

Unfortunately, being fair can get very complicated. Early in my career, when I had young children at home and very little time for anything except the children and painting, I solved the problem by saying to the inquiring client something like, "I'm sorry but I don't keep any work in my studio. It is all out in galleries and you must go through one of them to buy." That too became a nuisance because I found I was losing commissions. No one can talk to a client about a commission as well as the artist can. Things got even stickier when corporations began buying my

work. I *had* to open my studio at times to their agents. Finally I decided to use commercial galleries in other towns and to open my own personal gallery in my local area.

Budgeting
When I chose to open my one-artist gallery, I felt lucky to find a 400-square-foot space to sublet from another compatible business. Compatible businesses, in my mind, are decorating stores, furniture stores, art supply stores, etc. At the time, 400 square feet of sublet space seemed like a dream come true.

For that space in my small resort town in Florida, I paid $350 per month *rent* and a third of the *utilities* (since I had a third of the space). My utilities ran around $50 per month and that included keeping lights on in the display window all night. Utility prices can vary widely in different sections of the country.

One-hundred-fifty dollars per year went for *dues to the chamber of commerce*—a *must* for new businesses, since many contacts are provided by the chamber of commerce. Prorated, that amounts to $12.50 per month.

Business licenses vary in cost from area to area, too, and in my location they were too minimal to mention but, to avoid surprises, you should look into licensing before making any commitments.

Part-time help is another consideration you must make if you are embarking on my plan. You can't possibly be in your gallery every business hour and produce your work, too. I hired a person who was knowledgeable about art and who liked my work very much and who did not need to make a lot of money. I paid her minimum wage plus 10 percent of any sales she made, even if I happened to be standing beside her when she made the sale. I hardly ever was standing beside her because she worked two days per week and on those days I religiously stayed home and painted. Her salary before any commissions were

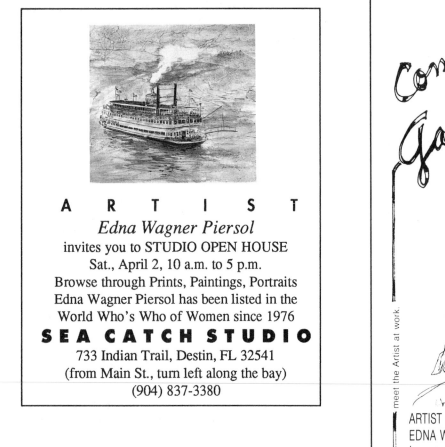

A R T I S T

Edna Wagner Piersol
invites you to STUDIO OPEN HOUSE
Sat., April 2, 10 a.m. to 5 p.m.
Browse through Prints, Paintings, Portraits
Edna Wagner Piersol has been listed in the
World Who's Who of Women since 1976

SEA CATCH STUDIO

733 Indian Trail, Destin, FL 32541
(from Main St., turn left along the bay)
(904) 837-3380

Here are two types of promotions I used for my gallery. Newspaper ads can be targeted at one date and time, so they're best used to advertise special events such as an open house. Multipurpose cards printed on heavy paper can be mailed as postcards and fit into racks at places like motels or the chamber of commerce.

meet the Artist at work.

ARTIST
EDNA WAGNER PIERSOL-WINDES
is proud to announce
the opening of

Sea Catch Studio

in Moreno Plaza
near the Destin Bridge

PORTRAITS—COMMISSIONS—ILLUSTRATIONS
(RENDERINGS TO YOUR LIKING)

BROWSERS WELCOME

(904) 837-3380

meet the Artist at work.

paid would be just under $250 a month.

My *advertising and telephone* budget was $200 per month. That allowed me only about two ads per month, minimal mailing, and no long-distance phone calls to speak of.

So my *total estimated expenses* came to $862.50 per month.

The commercial galleries that I am affiliated with (and they're all in towns at least 60 miles from my own gallery) take about 40 percent. Therefore, to make the same kind of profit on my work as I would in a commerical gallery, I'd have to make 60 percent gross profit, or $2,156.25 per month.

That figure rather frightened me until I realized that I often had sold that much at one-person shows, and that many of my paintings sold for a third of that figure and some sold for more than the total needed for a month's gross. I would just have to consider that I was having a one-person show every month. The sales required to accomplish my dollar goal broke down to an *average* of $88.01 per day based on being open six days per week (about 24.5 days per month). That meant on the days I was lucky enough to sell a couple of large commissions, I'd have several days when I could coast. But *never* to the point of not opening my doors. When the public is told that you will be open, you commit yourself to being *open*.

All this was before any 10 percent commissions were paid, but there didn't seem to be any good way to estimate how much my employee might sell, so I just felt I'd deduct those commissions from what I made and see how things went. After all, the more sold, the more I made, and those commissions only lowered my profits on *some* sales (those made by the employee) to 50 percent. In marketing, that's still a good "mark up."

Start-Up Considerations

There were, of course, some costs of starting up. I invested in:

- A sign for the front of the building — $250
- 1,000 four-color reproductions — $1,500
- 300 black-and-white repros of 20 x 30-inch drawings — $300
- New carpeting for display room — $650
- Wall remodeling and painting (my husband and I did most of the work) — $500
- Invitations and ads for the opening — $150
- Postage for the opening invitations — $50
- *Total opening-up investment* — $3,200

Everything but the postage will be useful for several years.

Some amenities, like an answering machine on a business phone number and a charge card set-up, I already had because I'd been running my home studio as a business for quite a while. You need to consider that your expenses will differ from mine.

Naturally, I needed a large stock of paintings of every kind and price range — enough to fill a whole gallery. I already had enough framed pieces to look good on the walls, but I set to work producing as many more small, matted things as I could. I never just toss off a painting with no regard to its quality. An artist can produce good "quick sale art" by adhering to sound composition and color rules and doing what the public likes in the artist's own way.

I thought perhaps a couple of reproductions would be a good idea to keep the cash flowing so I ordered a thousand four-color reproductions of one of my most popular paintings and then some black-and-white reproductions of drawings featuring local scenes. The reproduction idea did prove to be a good one. The reproductions were paid for by advertising and selling the first one hundred for a bargain price of $20 each. After that they sold for $35. They paid my expenses for many months.

The Results

My *expense estimate* turned out to be right, but not my *profit estimate* — I made a much larger profit than I'd expected, even after upping my part-time employee to about four days per week. The only explanation I can give is that people take an artist who has his/her own gallery very seriously. They buy more at higher prices. I soon found that I could afford more advertising and that, too, brought in more sales.

I even found a way to take a vacation or break every three or four months from my one-artist gallery. I simply arranged to lease out the gallery for a month during my break time. The leasing artist paid my rent and utilities for that month and paid for advertising. We advertised as though I were sponsoring a show for the leasing artist, but I made it clear in the lease/show agreement that the only real help I would give was an information sheet, stating newspaper ad deadlines, what form of advertising was most successful for me, and emergency phone numbers, etc.

Eventually I had to move from my sublet space. I thought that subletting inside another business would be fun, but I've since decided that it is better to be totally on your own. When you include yourself in an operation over which you have no control there can be problems on both sides. Even beyond conflicts of interest about business hours and the look of display areas and who used the most water or electricity there is the cold fact that an artist needs to attract a certain clientele and that another business involved—no matter how elegant it might be—can hurt those chances. I have now found that what I had in a subletting status, I can have on a smaller, more efficient scale on my own. Each artist's situation is different, of course, and situations do change.

I'm now ready to be on my own and I've learned a lot. I found 300 to 400 square feet is a good size for a gallery and that, for me, most of that space needs to be exhibit space, not work space. I found that I do not paint well at a place of business. The best I can do there, with all the interruptions, is put on a good show. My real work has to be done in my home studio. You may be different.

Guidelines for Your Gallery

I really am convinced that the possibilities of a one-person gallery are limited only by your ability to produce and your dedication to your boss, yourself. So here are a few guidelines.

When you are considering whether a one-artist gallery is a good plan for you, don't let my figures sway you either way. Don't just assume that you can or can't afford it. Check actual prices in your own area and when you find an appealing spot, go there for several consecutive

---

EDNA WAGNER PIERSOL/SEA CATCH GALLERY FOR

SUNDAY JUNE 21, 1988

Weather _____

Edna was in the gallery   yes_____ no_____

painting   yes_____ no_____

Virginia's hours were _____

Opening time _____

First sale _____

Total number of sales _____

Total number of customers _____

Last sale _____

Closing time _____

NOTES ON THE DAY _____

_____

_____

_____

A sales diary like this one can help you spot buying trends, allowing you to schedule your painting time during inactive periods in the gallery.

days and check out the traffic and other pros and cons in person. Talk to other business people in the area. Sitting at home and speculating is not very informative.

Other important elements you should consider are:

1. Good walk-in-off-the-street traffic is essential. Don't hide yourself on a back street. A good location is one near a restaurant and in a very "used" area, preferably used by people with money to buy art. Then you use the traffic to other businesses to your advantage by being open when most of the traffic is passing, or at least by using very visible display methods, including a prominent phone number on your door or window.

2. Make very certain that your desired business hours are in line with those of the location you are renting. Some shopping centers *require* certain open hours and they can be very long, like 9:30 a.m. to 9 p.m.

3. It is not always practical for the artist to work as a salesperson. I feel better with a hired person in my gallery—and now I know I can afford one.

4. Keep a guest book for your mailing list.

5. Keep a selling diary. Within three months you will know what days are great selling days and what day of the week could be your day off.

6. The *most important rule of all* is to put everything in writing and have it signed and dated. Starting with your rental lease and going on to every transaction you make—your leases with other artists, if you choose to lease out your space from time to time, any agreement you have with your landlord that is not covered by the lease, any agreement you make about advertising, and especially the sales agreements with your customers. Make up a little form instead of a sales slip that states what they have bought and what the terms are. Like "as is" or "not returnable" or "paid in full"—whatever is needed to make things easy on yourself. Especially get

time-payment agreements with your customers *signed by the customer*, stating at what point you will allow them to pick up the artwork, what monthly payments will be required, and the penalty for not paying.

Get a witness to sign large dollar-amount contracts and lease contracts, or better yet, get them notarized.

There are many forms you can use for these agreements including a simple letter signed by both parties. In most courts a paper signed by both parties is legal and you may be very thankful you have adopted this rule. *Don't ever disregard this rule of putting things in writing*, even when dealing with your best friend. A good way to get over your timidity in asking for signed contracts is to think, "Why would I want to deal with someone who is unwilling to sign an honest contract?"

7. The last rule for running a successful one-artist gallery is be prepared to work hard and expect the unexpected. Bad and *good*. After all, if you don't like this situation you can change it when your lease is up.

Alternative Galleries

If I had my way, I'd choose to have every artist set up in his/her own private one-artist gallery with a very good agent or salesperson to promote only that artist's work, but, of course, that is wishful thinking. Finding really good alternative space for exhibiting is what some artists have found to be the next best thing, especially if they have no commercial galleries near their living area. It can be almost as good as having one's own gallery, if the proper place is sought. Long ago I decided it was not good to exhibit in grocery stores—people shopping there do not have art on their minds. Hospital lobbies and hallways are often offered, but please don't expect people, with the weight of illness on their minds, or doctors, concerned for their patients' welfare, to generate many sales for you. Beauty shops and

Claire Justine
Artist
Shelbyville, Kentucky

When she lived in Marathon and San Angelo, Texas—where galleries can be few and far between—Claire Justine discovered the value of alternative galleries. Located in libraries, banks, universities, restaurants, and the like, these spaces can give artists exposure they might not find elsewhere.

Q. *How do you make use of alternative galleries?*

A. Galleries are few and far between in west Texas so alternative exhibiting spaces are a real joy to the local artists. I have had wonderful experiences with libraries, university galleries, business buildings, banks, and restaurants. The interesting thing is that patrons who view and purchase works from these places have very seldom been in a "real" art gallery. I have sold work through these outlets to doctors, a district attorney, lawyers, nurses, ranchers, and housewives.

One good example of the best of alternative exhibit spaces is The Library Gallery, in a Texas town where I used to live. The library building is a former department store. A long atrium runs through the middle of the building from one street to another. Across one of these streets are the county courthouse and the city hall plus several banks and office buildings. Across the street on the other side of the library building is the parking lot for all the people who work in all of these places. That causes traffic through the building all day long (a very important consideration for artists). Add to that traffic the library staff and patrons and you have a marvelous audience for your work. One side of the atrium contains the library itself and the other side has a long glassed-in gallery wall with the library office behind it. It is beautifully lighted to set off exhibits to the best advantage. Many people who have never bothered to go to a gallery opening view the exhibits here that change monthly. Exhibiting artists often have fantastic sales here. On the whole, because of the excellent exposure, I would choose to exhibit in the Library Gallery rather than at any of the other commercial galleries in that town.

Some alternative spaces have lovely gallery facilities like the one just described while others provide just a wall. The libraries, business buildings, and banks usually have someone responsible for selecting exhibits, inviting the artists, and choosing the dates, mostly done quite professionally—a big help for the artist. University galleries often have a waiting list and there is competition with students, regional, and even national artists for dates. The viewing audience at universities is sometimes more inclined to study, rather than buy, art and I have never found sales all that great. Artist friends of mine have had similar experiences.

Sometimes, the alternative exhibit spaces pay off big in ways you'd never suspect. Recently, one of these times came along during an exhibition of my collages. A busy lawyer, who had been viewing exhibits at the Library Gallery for several years, looking for just the right artist to execute a commission for him, told me he'd finally found the right one, in me. There were two conditions to this commission:

1. The title had to be "Legal Conflict." (The client was a boxing fan, as well as being a lawyer, and saw both of these fields as conflicts within a set of rules.)

2. The collage had to include a picture of his red Mustang—one of the original Mustangs—now beautifully restored.

It was a fascinating commission and one that I accepted with delight. It took quite a few months to collect and assemble the work, but when the collage was finally finished, I had completed a satisfying project and my client was thrilled with the product. Both his wife and his framer called to tell me so. Who says working on "someone else's idea" can't be creative?

To all striving artists I say: Look around you; there are opportunities to exhibit and sell your work everywhere. In alternative exhibit spaces, there is usually no commission charged because you handle all the paperwork. If the object of your work is ultimately to "show and sell," alternative spaces provide a great way to do it.

restaurants, although they get attention for the work, are too humid to be good for the condition of paintings.

An artist needs the same kind of situation for alternative exhibiting space as for a personal gallery—one that has a lot of foot traffic by the kind of people who have money to buy art. Lobbies at live theaters and banks may prove good. The lobby or hallway of a large office building has hope of sales and so does my favorite—space in a boutique—a space where people are already in the buying mode. These areas (and you will think of more, I'm sure) provide the kind of setting that enhances artwork and will give you, as an artist, a feel for how you can run your personal business of selling.

CHAPTER NINE

Choosing a Lifestyle

There are many career approaches open to an artist. Do you think you would like to sell your work through galleries? Or sit in an outdoor show and meet the public? Could you do that for a living? As we've seen, some artists make a substantial living that way. Or would you rather spend your life in academia? How about illustration? What does a commercial artist do? What other ways are there to make a living by wielding your brush? What are some of the lifestyles open to artists and what *does* the world want from us? We can try to find out by research. In this chapter I'll tell you a little about the lifestyle I chose when I began living by my brush alone and interview other artists about their lifestyles.

A Traveling Life

I wanted a traveling lifestyle, and I spent more than two years using my paintbrush to support my wanderlust. I didn't have to stop my itinerant ways and settle down. Maybe I haven't yet—I may take off at any minute. I discovered an artist can pretty much write her own ticket.

Travel! The love of my life! For years I had used every available chance to take long or short trips, but there were never enough chances. Now, divorced after twenty-six years of marriage and with my children grown, I wanted to avoid being tied to one area by a job. There were states I hadn't seen, and countries beckoning. Could I just pack my studio into my little brown car and take off, hanging a painting out the window with a sign stating: "For Sale for Supper"?

I'd always suspected you could make a living as an artist and live the kind of life you want without tying yourself to a nine-to-five job. Now I wanted to prove it.

Like most artists, I'd been "around" in the art world, paid my dues in various places: being a paste-up artist (before I married), then exhibiting in shows and "doing" the outdoor shows selling paintings—sometimes. But, never enough of anything to support myself as a painter.

Plan of Attack

So the first step was a drastic one. I brought back to my studio every painting that was out in a gallery unless it required shipping. I took most of the pictures out of their frames for easier packing. Then I sorted them into categories of things that might sell in various parts of the country: pelicans for Florida; horses for Kentucky and Indiana; figure sketches for Pittsburgh and Cincinnati, for example.

After sorting, I took a hard look at my records. What kinds of outlets had produced good results over the last two years? I thought of hitting the outdoor show trail because I'd had some success at it, but I wanted a different, more businesslike approach. Also, I did not want to plan my itinerary around places and times when outdoor shows would be available.

Fortunately, I had built up a small clientele, decorating and frame shops, who would buy outright from me. My little list of clients had been gained casually by dropping in on shop owners and showing a few paintings. These clients were in towns along a route I often followed when visiting friends and relatives. How could I build on this list to extend it so I could go where I wanted all over the country—maybe the world?

I decided on a three-pronged attack: (1) small decorating and framing shops, (2) department stores, and (3) large corporations.

I figured that if I painted hard for two weeks out of every month, and then went on a selling trip, I could make a living. I knew I could keep myself in one place for two weeks by renting cheap vacation cottages out of season and by staying with friends whenever possible. What I had to decide was whether I could sell my paintings. When I sold a framed painting to a gallery for $350, the gallery took 40 percent (some take even more). That left me with $210. The cost of producing a framed picture was at least $50, not to mention the shipping costs. I was left with $160 at most.

I was sure I could sell the same picture, unframed, for $160. So, what would I be losing? When traveling this way, a portion of gas, food, and lodging expenses is tax deductible (check with the IRS for specifics). It seemed worth a try. If it worked, I'd be going where I wanted to go, on one long "vacation," and deducting all my expenses.

I put together a presentation portfolio. I kept up with my expenses by calling people who had expressed interest in my work, making small, quick sales as I went. I found a certain amount of work produced a certain amount of money.

On the Road

When I felt ready, I headed for Indianapolis because it was a big city, yet small enough not to be too frightening. I arrived with just enough money for one night in a motel, food for one day, and a gasoline credit card. I had to sell.

In the Yellow Pages I found ads for two large department stores, and two or three ads for interior decorators and frame shops. Sometimes the latter buy original work and sometimes not. My phone calls were short and businesslike. I've found you should not put yourself into a subordinate position; you must be sure of yourself, so you are tactfully interviewing your prospective client. Find out if he buys art directly from an artist and if he sounds good for you. If he doesn't, then don't waste time! When a call goes sour, just scan the Yellow Pages for the next prospect.

From my calls I lined up two appointments for the next morning and two for the afternoon: a frame shop and a department store in the morning; decorators in the afternoon. (Decorators are hard to find in the morning; they are usually visiting clients.) My approach to frame shops and department stores is similar. First, phone for an appointment. The person you need to see is the buyer, who is usually located in the picture and mirror department. Don't be discouraged if, after an appointment is made, it takes a while to see her. Buyers are often busy and can't avoid being called out of their offices.

Joan Coate Milsom
Corporate Art Consultant
President of the Board of Directors
Pittsburgh Center for the Arts
Pittsburgh, Pennsylvania

When Joan Coate Milsom became president of the board of directors of the Pittsburgh Center for the Arts—the largest nonprofit art center in Pennsylvania with 1,700 member artists and a school with 4,000 students—and shortly after that took on a major corporate art-buying project, she found those jobs brought with them big changes in her lifestyle and her perspective.

Q. *You are a fine artist, and I know that you took the job as a corporate art buyer to expand your knowledge of painting, rather than to desert any part of your existence as an artist. How is it working?*

A. For most of my life, my soul has been involved with anything creative—mostly producing artworks, yet allowing my mind to sandwich into a full schedule the art classes and workshops needed to keep the creative juices flowing.

That creative routine was disrupted when I allowed myself to be thrust into the position with the Pittsburgh Center for the Arts. And, only six months after accepting that job, I was asked to become the art consultant for a 22-floor art-buying project for Blue Cross of Western Pennsylvania's new corporate building, under construction. I agreed, providing that I would buy only P.C.A. member artists' work. Now, everyone is profiting: Blue Cross, artists, and the center. To date Blue Cross has purchased from over one hundred twenty artists in all media and styles. When completed, this will be the largest single collection of Western Pennsylvania art in existence. A once-in-a-lifetime consulting position that consists of finding work of special quality, helping with a corporate catalogue, establishing an ongoing gallery of shows with artists from the collection, supervising the installation, as well as satisfying six art committees from the work force of Blue Cross, staying within a budget, and ending with the best possible collection that will please the Blue Cross personnel, the top executives, the customers, and myself. To say that this has been a challenge is very much a gross understatement.

Q. *What has buying for corporations taught you?*

A. Corporate buying has been a great teacher for me in learning how to: be patient; how to adjust to, cope with, and control emotions (mine and others); and it has taught me to appreciate everyone's viewpoint. Being immersed in so much art has also given me inspiration for that all important "next series" of my own creations.

Also, I was surprised to find that this artist's view, of art for art's sake, is not necessarily shared by the purchasers of art.

When you, as an artist, look at a piece of art that is not your own, you judge that work on its own merit. The artist's name is unimportant. That single visual interpretation is all that counts. Creative people are interested in studying other creations for stimulation and interest in new ideas. Each artist has an image of a successful creative unit that he applies to his own and others' work. If a piece doesn't measure up to your particular standards, it's a failure.

When first offered the opportunity to buy art for a corporation, the prospect of reviewing thousands of works by accomplished and recognized artists delighted me. But I soon found that the principles of buying art as an investment are contrary to the value judgments to which artists inside the art world adhere. The art which *most* corporations buy must act as decoration with investment as a secondary thought—an enhancing of the surroundings with, maybe, the potential to grow in value. The artwork must be in step with the corporation's image, keeping in mind that each corporation has its own personality. Therefore, I find myself looking at art in a new light. I had to examine the collective work of an artist to find consistent quality and constant progression. The idea is to buy work that will maintain or increase in value and still fit a particular corporate image.

Be patient and ready with your samples and wares. Make the most of your few minutes and be enthusiastic!

Just as with the phone calls, *I* try to do the interviewing. I stay pleasant, polite, and smiling, but I firmly decide if my work is right for this place. I stop wasting time as soon as I feel the buyer is not enthusiastic. I don't take offense if she's not interested.

By the end of my first day in Indianapolis, I'd made enough sales to assure my stay in town through the "Indy 500" (about a week). But, don't think it's always that easy. All calls do not produce sales. My average is one sale out of every three or four contacts. In Indianapolis I landed two big clients: a large department store and the biggest decorator in the area.

My courage was growing. I wanted to head still further from home—all those unvisited states and far countries were still calling me— but I felt the need to go to a place where I'd been before. I wanted to revisit Maine. But money was an issue again; how would I get there?

Maybe it was time for a big presentation to a corporation. I had the picture for it, a painting that had been too successful to sell unframed. It had been in several good shows, and I'd used it on my invitations and brochures. I knew the corporation collection I'd like it to be in. A telephone call to the art buyer for the corporation was politely received and an appointment was made. I told him the truth as enthusiastically as possible—that I had my most successful painting in town with me and, until now, had not been anxious to sell it. I explained that I was ready to have it become part of a good collection. Within a week my painting was sold and now belongs to the corporation. Success—and more courage.

Up to this point I had been living from day to day. This large sale turned me into a prudent soul again. I felt the urge to put most of the money in a bank against the day when I might need to pay my hospitalization or something similar. So I did, but I also called a friend in Maine and said I would be up to visit. By now I was confident I'd get money from somewhere. It sounds great to have friends to visit, but you must remember that there are gas, motels, and food to be paid for on the way. (I always think I'll eat "cheap" by going into grocery stores and buying inexpensive lunch meat and cheese. But I've been shocked into realizing that there is no such thing as *cheap* lunch meat and cheese.)

Teaching Classes

There was still another way of making money I had not yet explored. Several people wanted me to teach classes. A few phone calls told me I could hastily put together a small workshop. There wouldn't be many students, but there would be enough tuition to assure my being able to travel to the next place when I was ready.

A small group suited me fine for the Maine workshop. One student wanted to ride with me in my car and share expenses. Great! In my new lifestyle I didn't have to do things "big"; all I needed was enough to meet expenses.

The rest of my trip to Maine was financed by a student who bought two paintings from me when I informed her of the workshop plans. Talking and telling people about what I was doing proved to be a big asset. Sometimes we are too quiet about our hopes. My sales have been going well because I say that I want to sell, and I keep my prices reasonable.

I certainly don't give my work away, although I've done some bartering. I've traded a painting for work on my car, and one for a place to stay the night—for legal advice and dental work, too.

In Maine I never passed up an opportunity to sell. One morning I went to the beach to paint, and a woman came up to watch me. After a few minutes she told me that the gift shop at Fifth and Main would be interested in my work. I used to just thank people for this kind of information and say I'd check it out later. Not anymore!

When someone gives me information on prospective clients, I take time to talk to this person as I did with the woman on the beach. How reliable was she? What was her purpose in telling me about the shop? You'll probably find out a lot if you ask her if you can use her name when calling on the new client. The shop *was* interested—$300 worth of sales!

When the Maine interlude was over, I headed for Washington, D.C., where my mail caught up with me. There were two letters from far-away cities, both unvisited places, and both gave promise of future work. Living by my paintbrush was fun!

Update

Since those days, I have settled down—at least to living in one spot—mainly because I met and married a man who stimulates my mind and understands the moods of an artist. As you have read, I even opened a gallery of my own for a while. One of the biggest thrills of my life was arriving at my gallery one morning to find a young woman artist and her husband asleep in their car in the parking lot. They had been doing a long-distance night drive to his new job in Texas and had seen my name on the gallery sign in the middle of the night. They'd waited for me so I could sign her copy of one of my books. I didn't refuse.

The love of travel will always be with me and I still find ways every year to let my career help me ride my paintbrush around the world, teaching workshops, doing portraits and art consulting jobs, and sometimes just painting by the roadside. Once you learn that you·can live by your brush alone and let it take you where you want to go, the habit is hard to break.

When You Need a Job

J. Price Wiesman, an artist from Smyrna, Georgia, whose views on marriage between artists you will read on page 100, told me about a positive change in her lifestyle as an artist, brought about by necessity—a blessing in disguise. She said that a few years ago a job setback put her under financial pressure, and she faced some tough decisions about her art.

"The basic truth about being an artist is that one can paint for self-expression, to sell, or to win awards," she says. "Ideally one paints for the first reason and the others ensue. However, as financial obligations increase, it is sometimes hard to adhere to the first goal and there is a temptation to paint toward what you know will sell rather than look into a nine-to-five job out of your field, or starve." She was hesitant to take a job outside the art field because experience had shown such jobs robbed her of the creative energy for painting.

"Our finances were suffering so that the possibility of painting for money and not art seemed imminent. That might end my career, too. I looked for solutions every day in classified ads and through conversations and fortunately the solution for me came along." She landed a job at Georgia Tech Research Institute as the artist responsible for graphic supports. "During the day my brush becomes a 'mouse' while my canvas is a computer screen."

Wiesman says the job stimulates, rather than stifles, her creativity. "Being in charge of technical presentations and illustrations has finely honed my drawing skills as well as the other elements of basic design. The job was created for me and I was hired as the first artist to work with research engineers in this laboratory. My work has provided an exciting and stimulating challenge and kept me actively creative during the day and ready to explode my canvas with color during the evening. This situation has worked well for me; it might not for everyone. But I now feel that I have the luxury of creativity in its purest sense. I am probably painting better than I ever have before and starting to truly establish myself in fine arts. And yes, I do receive creative satisfaction in my daytime job. I've seen some of my briefings travel to the Pentagon, Brussels, Austria, Japan, and even China. My drawings have appeared in technical publications/magazines both in the U.S. and France."

Many artists share Wiesman's view that a job outside the art world drains some creativity. Others feel that an art-related job does the same thing—for instance, that a job as an advertising artist will keep you from becoming an exhibiting artist. I think it is an individual decision. For myself, I've found that I can only really work at an art-related or otherwise creative job. Any noncreative kind of job bores me to the point where

I will fail. Fortunately for me, besides painting commissions, there are many creative jobs available (if I choose to take one), such as writing. When all else fails, I have often fallen back on walking the streets to drum up clients. I haven't starved yet, but I'm thankful for the day that I finally said to myself, "Hey, you don't really have to do *anything* but make pictures and sell them." That's when I really began living by my brush alone.

"Hotel in Ocean Grove, NJ," Edna Wagner Piersol, 30 x 40 inches, watercolor.

I traded this painting for room and board at this hotel.

CHAPTER TEN

Business Sense

The minute you sell a painting, you are a business person, whether you like it or not. The more businesslike you are, the more profit you'll make.

There are pitfalls in the business of being an artist. One of them is that you must trust your work to others so often. What happens if a gallery goes bankrupt after you have consigned your work there? It depends on the laws of the state where you are living and working. It is entirely possible that, unless you take precautions and get signatures on various legal forms before leaving your work, you could *lose* your paintings in the event the gallery goes into bankruptcy. It sounds unfair, and it is. Bankruptcy laws in some states are unclear, so be forewarned. Artists' Equity Association of America, Inc. (P.O. Box 28068, Central Station, Washington, D.C. 20038) has information about this and many other problems and is a good organization to join. As an artist on your own, you need all the information you can find to keep your work safe.

At this writing, very few states exempt artists from the laws governing consigned goods. Bankruptcy laws are designed to protect creditors, and consigned property is usually judged to be an asset of the bankrupt gallery, even though it is still owned by the artist. In some states, such as Florida, a form can be obtained from the Secretary of State of Florida which, if signed *before* consigning your work to the gallery, assures that your work will not be classified as part of the gallery's assets.

It is a good policy to review your records each month and remove gallery paintings and replace them with new ones every sixty days or so. That keeps you in touch with the gallery, and gives you a feeling for what is happening. If no paintings have been sold in sixty days, it is likely the gallery is not going to produce well anyway. Give them a reason why you want to take all of your work out temporarily, and later you can return the paintings or submit new ones. Keep the inventory of paintings in the gallery low until you feel good about the establishment. Why take unnecessary risks?

Copyright

Copyright laws are another area that you should explore and get to know well. Today, the copyright laws in the United States state that the copyright of a painting belongs to the artist who produced it from the moment of its creation, unless the artist *signs* away his copyright. (A copyright can only be transferred in writing.) In other words, as long as an artist does not sell the copyright along with the work, the right to make money by reproducing it or by selling the reproduction rights to it belongs to the artist.

It is always a good idea to place your copyright notice (a *c* with a circle around it © followed by the year date and your name or an abbreviation by which your name can be recognized) on your paintings and slides, even though you have not yet officially registered your copyright with the copyright office. Official registration need not take place until an actual infringement of your copyright takes place; however, to be eligible to collect attorney fees and statutory damages (to be compensated for the infringement) the registration must occur within three months of the painting's publication. To further understand copyright, write or call the U.S. Copyright Office (U.S. Copyright Office, Library of Congress, Washington, D.C. 20559, 202-287-8700) and obtain the free Copyright Information Kit. Books on copyright are also available at your library.

Pricing Savvy

What to charge for work is always a puzzle. I can't count the times a student has asked me that question. The answer is that one artist's worth does not depend on that of any other artist. The price of your paintings is determined by the quality of your work and the strength of your name. Since the general public has a hard time believing in its own judgment, the strength of your name is important. Start out by noting what other artists are charging for comparable work. Check outdoor shows and galleries that carry new names. Set your prices accordingly. From then on, try whatever price the market will bear. If you are not getting as much money per painting as you think you should, look for reasons other than price. Maybe you are not in your right market. Another gallery or art center may be better for you.

Never lower a price if you can avoid it. If you *must* do it, do it in a way that will not become common knowledge. For instance, tell the person in charge of sales that it will be all right to sell your paintings at *X* number of dollars less than the marked price, provided it is done quietly. That way, the public will have your original price as an example of the quality of your work. You may find that you need to raise your prices. If a potential buyer notices that a price has gone up, he may assume that the overall value of the artist's work has gone up.

There are psychological prices. People who will pay $125 for a painting will not pay $100. One thousand dollars is a bad price; $1,500 is good. I don't know why psychological prices exist. Perhaps the subconscious of the buyer tells him that if an artist wants $100 for a painting, it is an arbitrary figure; but if the artist wants $125, the price has been figured out by an evaluation of cost.

As I mentioned earlier, never, under any circumstances, take a painting out of the gallery or show in order to sell it cheaper to a client. Sometimes an opportunistic buyer will suggest that you do this and split the gallery commission with him. Don't. Always discuss your sales with the gallery or show chairman and always pay the commission. You need the goodwill of those agents who sell for you.

When dealing with galleries or the public, your pricing savvy can be based on this marketing rule: The wholesaler doubles the manufacturer's price; the retailer doubles the wholesale price. You are both manufacturer and wholesaler. If a gallery buys a painting from you outright for $100, they should sell it for about $200.

If you sell a painting outright to a gallery, you lose all control over the final price. If the gallery can sell it for $300 instead of $200, they have the right to keep the extra money. Yet, that can work to the artist's advantage in terms of cash flow. When I need money, I often make an offer to a gallery or decorator, enabling them to buy two or more paintings at a reduced rate, with the stipulation that they must be sold at my regular retail price. This deal keeps my public price up, keeps the gallery happy, and gives me the money I need, instead of waiting for the paintings to sell to receive payment.

Usually a gallery won't buy outright, but will want to take a painting on consignment and make only a 40 percent commission. Then you will get $120 (if it sells at $200) instead of the $100.

If you prefer to judge the final price of your paintings by an hourly pay scale, figure the hourly rate you want. Add it, multiplied by the hours you have worked on the painting, to the cost of materials.

Example: You want to work at $10 per hour. You've worked five hours on the painting, and the materials cost $50. You will want to wholesale the painting for $100 ($105 is better).

It might be helpful to use an estimating form, like the one that follows, to help you gauge your pricing when you are talking to a prospective buyer about a commission. Do not give a price off the top of your head. Instead, find out what the client wants: size, type of pigment, and the time limits placed on you. Go back to your studio and figure out the cost of the commission in an organized way. Then give the client a solid price, based on cost and your markup for time. We artists are not very realistic creatures, so it is good to have a few forms to fill out in order to make our heads control our imaginations.

A sample estimation for a painting done on commission follows:

Materials and Time		Cost
1. Paper, canvas, or other support (add in an extra piece for the failures)		$ 10.50
2. Colors	6 tubes at $2.00	12.00
3. Hours spent painting	5 at $10.00	50.00
4. Research hours	2 at $10.00	20.00
5. Research material	2 rolls film plus developing (list all here)	18.00
6. Mat and frame materials	(list all here)	45.00
7. Matting and framing hours	2 hours at $10.00	20.00
8. Plexiglas	1 piece	23.00
9. Delivery charge (also include gas for research and parking fees, etc.)	$0.27 per mile (15 miles)	4.05
10. Add 100 percent profit (This is called a 50 percent markup)		$202.55
		202.55
		$405.10

Round off this price to your customer to $415 (sounds better than $405.10.) Or have the courage to go to $425. I would.

Bookkeeping Basics

Setting up your books as a business person is a must. If you have an accountant or one in the family, you are lucky. If not, my simple set of books should serve you for a long time. The main thing to remember is that you must keep detailed records of sales and expenses plus *proof* of these transactions. Get information from the Internal Revenue Service about what records you will need and start from there. (Consult your telephone book for the number and location of your nearest IRS office. Most IRS information is now handled by telephone or by mail.)

My "books" consist of inexpensive student composition books with wire binders. On the front I write "Tax Records—(Year)" in bold magic marker. Head the first page *January, (year)* for a written record of the sales for January. Make columns for date/amount/client/payment arrangement. On the second page I glue proof of those transactions, i.e., gallery slips, sales slips,

check stubs, etc. Three or four pages are left blank for more sales slips. Then on page five or six, I write a record of expenses for January—date/amount/type of purchase/store, and any other pertinent data. On the following pages, I glue the sales slips and receipts that are proof of purchase.

The composition books are flexible enough to allow almost any expansion caused by the sales slips. No slip gets away as it might if you were sticking it into a folder. The last page for each month is a written recap of the month.

The only other records I keep are my checkbook and savings account book. When I make a deposit, I record in the bank book the name of the client from whom the payment came. If I need to transfer from one account to another, I make a note by the deposit: "from savings" or "from checking." Never make a deposit without some notation to show its source. Try to purchase everything, including supplies or even postage, by check. If you're forced to pay cash, make a note in your checkbook of the transaction. I make these notes on the date that a check would have been written. That way I never miss

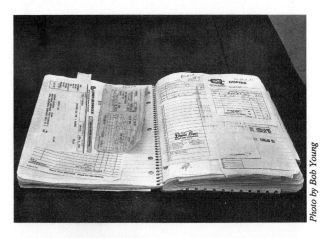

Photo by Bob Young

I simply tape receipts that I'll need for tax records onto the pages of a spiral notebook. This keeps the proof of my transactions in one place, easily accessible, and organized by month.

any expenses. The composition book records and sales slips serve as a backup.

Paying Yourself

Do you want the stability of a salary? It's fairly easy to set one up. First, face the fact that there will be long periods of time when you won't make money. Plan ahead. Start a "cash flow savings account,"—one that has no penalty for withdrawals—or use a money market checking account. (Consult your accountant or local bank.) You may have to draw out fairly large sums each time so as to avoid paying a penalty. (You can always put some back immediately.) Put every check or payment you receive into this cash flow account. Borrow to start the account if necessary. Simply pay yourself a certain set amount at the first of each month. You may have to do some budget revising in the beginning, but if you pare your living expenses down to a minimum and do a lot of planning about how you are going to make your money, you should have the hang of it in a month or two.

Once I adjusted to living as an artist, I set up my salary another way. I sold as many paintings as possible on time payments. Five or six payments of over $100 coming in per month go a long way toward meeting expenses. Time payments without using a credit card give both you and your client an advantage. The client does not pay interest, which saves him a lot of money if he is paying for a $3,000 painting. The advantage for you is that you might not have made the sale otherwise, so what are you losing? Be careful, though; once I almost lost the last $200 of an $1,800 sale because I forgot to get the client's signature. The buyer had paid me $1,600 and said he'd send the balance in a month. After six months my lawyer wrote him—fortunately this worked and he paid.

Set up your time payment sales the following way. On memo slips or sales slips from an office supply store, write the client's name and address,

the item purchased, and details such as "unframed" or "as is" or "plus shipping." *Be sure you get the signature of the client on this.* Once that is done, you are pretty well protected.

If you decide to make credit card sales available to clients, call your bank—they handle merchant accounts and can give you the information you need, so that people may charge their purchases with you on a credit card.

Benefits and Taxes

Since you will be working for yourself, you will have to supply your own health insurance and retirement fund. Don't neglect this. Include them in your budget for the year. Shop around for health insurance, and do check various art groups to see if an insurance plan is available for members. Talk to your bank and your insurance company about retirement options. Buy insurance immediately, at the earliest age possible, to get the best breaks. Whatever age you are, you'll never be any younger, so don't put it off.

When selling from your home studio, you will probably need a sales tax number, which also provides you with sales tax exemption on your art supplies. If you sell all of your work through galleries, you still need a tax number if you want to get the exemption on your supplies. Obtain tax information from your state tax office and the Internal Revenue Service and comply with it. You may also need a business license. Call your local government office to find out what's needed in the way of licenses or permits.

An accountant is invaluable at tax time. Your taxes as a self-employed business person are a little complicated, as you will see when you get your tax information. Your accountant isn't a miracle worker, so organize your information as well as you can. I never give mine the Tax Record composition book—that's for my eyes only. Instead I turn over to my accountant a neatly written single sheet of paper showing *all* my expenses and sales for the year. The expenses must be broken down into certain categories. (Check with her in advance to see how she wants it done.) The categories may change from year to year, but a few to remember are: *Utilities* — if you use one room of a six-room house for studio space, you can deduct one-sixth of your utilities. Keep a separate list of utility charges. (If an artist wants to claim home office/studio space as a deduction, he must have a specific space that is used *regularly* and *exclusively* for his trade or business. It may be the artist's actual dwelling or a nearby separate structure used for business, but personal and business efforts must be kept separate.)

You can deduct *car expenses* by keeping track of mileage used for your business; a rate per mile is allowed. *Professional fees* — exhibition fees and membership fees must be listed separately. *Art supplies* — purchased art supplies may be lumped together, but *books* should be kept separate.

There are other tax considerations your accountant will be able to tell you about; leasing a car might be advantageous. There are times when you may want to defer a client's payment. Talk over such matters with your accountant.

Banking Your Business

You need all the financial information you can get when starting a business. Make an appointment with your bank. Sit down and tell them what you are doing — setting yourself up in business as an artist. Be frank about how much, or how little, money you have. You may be surprised at how helpful a bank can be. If it disappoints you, try another bank. They can tell you exactly how to set up your savings accounts, checking accounts, and retirement plans to your best advantage. They will probably give you a work sheet to figure out your assets, and tell you the kinds of loans for which you qualify. It is well worth a morning's time. Business is business and art is art — but the two must meet.

Barter

Don't be afraid to live by your talent in any honest way. Barter is a way that you might make up to three-fourths of your income. In a shaky economy, it may be a more likely way to get you what you need than by other means.

Living space is one thing that you might obtain this way. Once, while completing a project, I toyed with the idea of advertising in the *Wall*

"Ghost of Freedom," Edna Wagner Piersol, 48 x 40 inches, acrylic on masonite.

This cowboy almost turned into a Volkswagen when a young man offered his car in exchange for the painting. But I didn't need an extra car at the time. Bartering works best when you trade for things you're ready to buy.

Randy McGovern
Wildlife Artist
Atlanta, Georgia

As you can see by the photo taken while fishing, Randy McGovern is a man who has his cake and eats it too. It is obvious that he gets his wildlife information first hand. He is an avid fisherman and outdoorsman, a hunter with a camera. Many of his most pleasurable working days are spent gathering data and experience for later paintings which has resulted in his becoming one of the bestselling wildlife artists in the Southeast, operating a business that sells reproductions and originals, nationally and internationally as far east as Japan and as far south as Columbia.

Q. *Besides selling your original paintings, you sell beautiful reproductions. When and how did you get started in selling reproductions?*

A. I first began my transition to full-time professional wildlife artist toward the end of 1982 when a friend, Brad Thompson, invited me to paint with him full time, sitting in Clearview Mall, Metairie, Louisiana. I said "O.K.,"

quit my secure job as draftsman, and on January 1, 1983, we began to share a generous amount of space leased to us by the mall. We split the rent, the display panels, and the twelve-hour shifts—six hours each. Everything was "uphill." I only had a few originals and a couple of black-and-white prints that I hand colored. The mall would not allow us to sell during store hours, but customers did come back after hours to pick up their pictures.

Eventually, after a few months I had saved up enough to order a color print done. One print led to another and after ten and a half months, I was finally working full time out of my home studio. It wasn't exactly by choice. By that time the mall had taken our space away. Adversity is often a blessing, though. The loss of mall space forced me to stop doing local scenes and I went national with what I'd always wanted to do—reproductions as a way to market my talent.

Lest anyone think this all sounds easy—it was not. There is a lot of inventory that has to be on hand when you go into business. For me it was not only paintings but wire and molding for frames. Everything from the film for your camera, before you even start to think about subjects, to the sticker labels that go on the back of your pictures—all cost money. I used some vacation money that I'd saved up, and fortunately, I had some good help from family members who became "employees." We grossed enough in the first year to meet expenses and make a living for myself and two "employees." I must say, though, that our salaries were meager and life was like a juggling act.

Q. *How did you find a printer for your works? And do you publish them yourself or work under the auspices of an art publisher who* *pays you a royalty?*

A. I publish myself. I've used several printers around the country. Good printers are not hard to find and the best ones are not necessarily the most expensive, although there is some truth the the adage that you get what you pay for. The best idea is to find a printer whose price policies you feel comfortable with, in close proximity so that you can watch the prints as they come off the press and thereby add priceless input.

Q. *But how do you find a printer? Look in the Yellow Pages?*

A. You could do that and start calling, but it's a better idea to talk to other artists about printers, paper, and prices. The quality of your print is very important and all this goes into it. When we started, we called a printer in Minneapolis and asked advice on paper to use. I'd call Minneapolis the Wildlife Art Capital of the World. There are probably one hundred full-time wildlife artists there and many printers who are familiar with the art and the publishers as well as the shows. Minneapolis is also a very crowded market for wildlife art.

Q. *Which method, self-publishing or finding a publisher, do you think is best for an artist and why?*

A. I've always published my own work, though I've had numerous offers from publishers. By publishing my own work, I may have sacrificed a little clout in some circles, but that is eclipsed by the joys of artistic autonomy and a much greater profit potential. (Publishers make most of the money on a "print"—but they do bear the printing and marketing expenses.) Still, in my opinion, self-publishing is the way to go if you can afford it.

Q. *What advice do you have for artists who would like to make some money selling reproductions?*

A. Concentrate, first and foremost, on the quality of your painting. Wait for your best work and push it to perfection. Only then should you print.

The professional offset-litho reproduction market is very competitive and there are too many amateur prints sitting on shelves around the country. Remember your chief motive for printing is not only to share the beauty of your art, but to make a profit. Consider, also, your subject matter in relation to your market. More Americans seem to want a picture of a Wood Duck than a Bohemian Wax Wing.

Q. *What allowances toward reproduction do you make in applying your paint to originals? Do you use brighter colors? More contrast? What if anything do you do to make paintings reproduce better?*

A. While painting, I'm always conscious of the fact that in a balanced print job my colors will lose brightness, so I do make allowances for that. The time to worry about contrast is when the prints are coming off the press and the printer is adjusting the black ink. I'm a fanatic about dust particles, especially on dark areas. I spend hours with tweezers getting dust off the painting when I'm preparing to have color separations made. Seventy-five percent of printing success is getting a good color separation.

Q. *Then how do you go about marketing your work?*

A. Sitting in the mall, I had begun to perceive that reproductions would sell well. Now when I'm sitting and painting at a show, I start to take orders on the prints of the painting on which I'm working and in that way I do my own market research. If the painting is going to do well in reproduction, I will have most of my printing money up front, and that's great because printing does cost a lot!

I do a lot of sitting and painting at trade shows and sports shows, etc., but at least one-half of my business is wholesale to galleries. That helped tremendously to get my name before the public and did wonders for my so-called popularity. I feel galleries are the artist's best friend. For me, advertising in decorating trade magazines has helped to find galleries.

Q. *What other suggestions have you for new artists?*

A. Organize your studio continually to assure peak efficiency. Remember *time* is *paintings*. Be ever conscious of the fundamentals: good drawing, good composition, light play, and execution of detail. Know yourself and your painting. If you are an impressionist; don't overwork it. If you are a realist; don't underwork it. Be sensitive and teachable in your attitude toward the public's reaction to your art. You can learn a lot from the average guy on the street.

Finally, be a smart businessman or woman and treat others fairly.

Street Journal for living space in exchange for artwork of any kind. I didn't have to go that far. An acquaintance put a house at my disposal in exchange for artwork. It's odd that as soon as that happened, I began to feel as though I was taking advantage of my friends. That was silly. I've come to realize that people do not offer things unless they want to do so. Artists are special to many people; being able to be a part of an artist's creativity is an honor to them. It's a genuine feeling.

Sometimes you can suggest the barter and other times your clients will suggest it. It can come as a delightful surprise. My large painting of a cowboy titled, "Ghost of Freedom" had been on exhibit in a restaurant for a week, when I received an urgent call from a young man who wanted to trade his Volkswagen for the painting. I didn't need an extra car, so he lost out. Another time, when I needed caps on my teeth, my dentist was amenable to a trade. Be careful when you do this. Try to avoid deals that could have disastrous results. You don't have much recourse when you're having teeth fixed. It worked out well for me and probably will for you too, but give it due thought before you act.

Thinking creatively about bartering can sometimes get you out of a "got ya" situation. J. Price Wiesman, who you met on page 85 and will meet again on page 100 tells the following story. Her daughter Cheri's pet Amazon parrot, Precious, was ill and the veterinarian told them it required surgery. "The medical bills were going to be *quite* expensive," Weisman recalls. "It was then I had an inspiration. I had just finished a vividly colorful painting of a parrot and I now offered to trade it to the vet for the surgery. He happily agreed. There are a lot more parrot paintings in my portfolio now—in fact some of my best paintings are of parrots and other exotic birds."

Another bartering situation from Weisman shows how far you can go with it. One situation often builds on another. She received a commission from a property developer to paint the Concord Covered Bridge, a historical landmark soon to be the namesake for his newest subdivision. He wanted the painting as an illustration for the subdivision brochure. "As artists we all strive for perfection, but every once in a while, do you ever amaze yourself with a truly special piece of work? That's what happened to me this time," Weisman says. "I became sorry that it was a commission. I wanted to keep it." Weisman suggested that instead of paying her for the commission, the developer finance a limited edition reproduction of the painting to be printed along with the brochure. He agreed. Since she had no reproduction costs, her budget allowed for packaging of the reproduction and a brochure to be used to market the reproduction. Weisman says, "Most important, I now have several new ways of getting my work out before the public. Not only do I have good new brochures to pass out at shows and in general with business cards, I have an inexpensive reproduction to sell as a bread-and-butter item that often pays all my expenses at art shows and I benefit by the builder's use of my painting in his subdivision brochure. As an outgrowth of this I am now working with community groups creating note cards of local scenes, receiving still more public exposure for my work."

Barter opportunities are everywhere. Do you need body work done on your car? Maybe the owner of the shop would like a good painting of his business place to use in advertising. Better yet, he might like a painting of his favorite car. Do you need display space for your paintings? Try approaching the owner of a boutique with the offer of doing her portrait for the space you'd like. Once I traded sailing lessons for drawing lessons. Do you need typing or editing done? Try trading. Is there a grocery store owner in your area who has several children and would like portraits in exchange for groceries? If you arrange a few barter agreements before you set out to support yourself by artwork, you can gain a little sense of security.

Remember, barter is income. You must report it to the Internal Revenue Service. You have to set a fair, provable value on what you are trading, as does the person with whom you are trading. There must be written proof of the value of the item. (Contact the IRS for more details.)

When bartering, be sure to get a written agreement. It may not be necessary for little things or quick one-time exchanges, but if going into something like a living arrangement, it is best to get a lease.

You have probably guessed that barter works much better with small business owners and individuals than large corporations. It would be silly to try to trade a portrait for a share of AT&T—but who knows?

Photo by Jack Collins, Smyrna, Georgia

"Parrot Bright," J. Price Wiesman, 20 x 24 inches, watercolor.

J. Price Wiesman once traded a painting of a parrot to a veterinarian in exchange for expensive surgery for her daughter's pet parrot. Since then she's done several paintings of parrots.

Virginia Stallings
Graphic Artist
Highland Heights, Kentucky

Virginia Stallings is currently the coordinator of the Northern Kentucky University communications lab, where students learn to design and create camera-ready art for everything from brochures to newspaper ads to business cards and hone their skills in typesetting, design, and layout. Unlike her students, Stallings got into commercial art without formal training. She has worked for a weekly newspaper, created her own job at a department of state government, and run her own advertising agency. Here she talks about what's needed to break into commercial art.

Q. *How does an artist become a commercial artist? Can you do it without attending a commercial art school?*

A. While I have managed rather well without benefit of college or commercial training in art and design, I cannot help but wonder where I might have gone with training. That is one of the reasons I enjoy my present job so much; I can strongly urge students to gain all the education possible about their craft *before beginning*. I can help students skip the years that I spent stumbling through—experimenting—to accomplish the effects that I desired. For instance, one of my most exciting discoveries, "back when," was press-on type. To be able to capture the mood I wanted in an ad by simply pressing the lettering onto the paper, playing with the letters, tipping them, tumbling them around the artwork—was mind-boggling. Had I had the training I urge upon others, I'd have had access to that sort of material much earlier. The "tricks of the trade" would have been shared.

Q. *What was your first job in commercial art and how did you get it?*

A. I began in advertising as a sales rep in a small Michigan weekly newspaper, and that proved to be invaluable training for commercial art and advertising in general because I discovered that my sales soared when I created specific ads to suit my customer's needs, rather than using stock ads.

Q. *Tell us about how you created your own 9-to-5 job after you left the newspaper.*

A. When I moved to another state, with my newspaper background, I found a job as a reporter in the state's Public Information Department but soon found myself suggesting a better way to advertise programs and services by translating private-sector commercial advertising practices to public services. My art abilities were soon put to use in my new job when the Art Unit was created to serve that department of state government and I was put in charge. I think that an artist's mind will create, and it can create a job as well as it can create anything else.

Q. *What does freelancing in commercial art entail?*

A. Commercial art is a generalization for all the art needed in the printing and publishing of information, the advertising and sign-painting industry, plus any other display art, etc. — in other words, any art that is not fine art, not displayed and sold in galleries and museums. In this age of computers and television the possibilities are almost endless. I did break in "through the back door," which is still possible, but some training really helps. Freelancing means that you are self-employed, working on your own for clients of your own seeking and choosing. It is hard work but the rewards are all for you, not shared. So are the rejections, so you must learn to be tough.

Q. *What is the most important thought you could pass on to an aspiring commercial artist?*

A. It is most important to let your mind do the work in the same way as a computer would. Mentally enter all the important information and allow your brain to explore and create. Think of the variety of approaches to a project that you may use, discarding none. Put your ideas on paper: design here, copy (words) there, then play. Allow your unconscious mind to do the work while directing your conscious mind and your hands and eyes to pull it all together.

Back at the beginning of my career, in my insulated world at the newspaper, I was competing with the big boys at the daily press for advertising. The stress of the competition and their disdain for a woman (this was a while ago) were tremendous. My ability to play with my ideas and know that I was "individual" probably made me successful. My ideas were my biggest weapon. Don't underestimate your mind.

Between stints of working for other people, Virginia Stallings ran her own advertising agency specializing in logo design, among other things. This was the logo for the firm, Ad Design Company.

CHAPTER ELEVEN

Can Marriage Survive an Artist?

Artists are like everyone else. Some live alone and like it; some live alone and *don't* like it. Some live together as husband and wife, or whatever, and like it; some live together and *don't* like that. None of us can help but be deeply affected by those who live with or near us. Does this condition affect artists more than others? Based on my own experience, it seems this might be true. In discussing the problem with a variety of people, both artists and nonartists, I was amazed at the interest the subject evoked. Each time this subject comes up when I'm conducting a workshop or seminar, I worry about the advice that I must be giving through body language. I bite my tongue so as not to put it into words, but I'm sure it shows in my eyes. I don't want to be the one who tells an artist who is struggling with a disappointing marriage the cold fact of life that each artist, or pair of artists, or artist's spouse must face—that art is the worst rival a lover can have. No one can love an artist without knowing this. What we do with that knowledge is the test of fire for the artist, as well as the mate.

I've noticed that there doesn't seem to be much middle ground for artists; they are either too self-centered or too giving. Some artists bend over backwards to *not* be selfish, and find themselves torn between their love for art and their love for their families. For instance, an artist who has to support a family may feel unable to dedicate his or her life to art. Or a parent may find a child's demands taking precedence at a crucial time in a career. It seems the self-centered artists or the ones who have found a mate who makes them the center of the universe are the ones who succeed.

But I've felt another side of this coin, too. During periods when I was in the most stressful situations, I was the most productive artistically.

It seems to me that the issue of how a career in art affects marriage and family life deserves more exploration. On that premise, I screened the results of many conversations and came up with the following insights into what makes or breaks a marriage of creative people.

J. Price Wiesman
Artist married to Musician
Atlanta, Georgia

Q. *Both you and your husband, Bob, have active, creative careers. What do you think has made your "artistic" marriage work?*

A. After twenty-one years of marriage, we feel that not only can a marriage survive an artist or two, but is, if anything, easier for us because one of the major causes of divorce has been eliminated—boredom, being in a rut. We have a "mixed marriage": performing and visual arts. Therefore, we do not compete with each other. While Bob has his undergraduate degree in design, his life is music. On the other hand, I have a strong music background in piano and violin, but would rather "paint than pick." Early in our marriage we did have some problems. I wanted Bob to paint more. He is capable of excellent work. Bob wanted me to "learn fiddle" and perform with him. We soon came to realize that we both were happier pursuing our own interests while supporting each other's.

Bob is the chief and best critic of my completed work, as well as my organizer and marketing planner. I am continually amazed at his ability to do all this, plus his ability to perform, to play literally any instrument with strings. I still, always, enjoy his performances. Bob gets the worst of the deal. There are a lot more paintings to pack, load, and unload when I'm doing a show, than [there are] instruments and sound equipment when he is doing a performance.

With the addition of a family, our situation expanded. We always knew that any children of ours would either love or hate art and music, but would never be indifferent to them. Since the age of two, the girls have been performing with their Dad and now, at the ages of fifteen and seventeen, are seasoned entertainers with "The Wiesman Family Singers." Recently, there has been a change in the family act. Formerly, Bob would completely plan the show—songs, arrangements, everything. Now, the planning has a three-person input with the girls also announcing what numbers they wish to perform, who will sing the lead, and who will play what instrument. In this part, I enjoy remaining in the background and find it hard to keep a straight face at times.

At this point in our marriage there has been another wonderful union. Our daughters have combined both Bob's interest in music and my interest in art by becoming involved in the Cobb Children's Theater and not only acting but doing set design running lights and sound equipment, working backstage as "grips," handling props, even working on costuming—marrying art to music marvelously. The ultimate joy was their sharing in the production of "Peter Pan" in which Cheri played Wendy, while Teri played Michael, Wendy's little brother. Music interests for the girls don't end at the theater. They enjoy contemporary gospel singing and singing in church services of all kinds. On the art side, Cheri has

built up quite a following for her face painting at "my" art shows.

As might be gathered, with all our interests, we seem to be continually on the go. Sometimes we wonder when we will actually have a night at home, with nothing planned, to just relax. But do we really want that? Even long trips are easy with everyone singing and playing instruments on the road.

In summation, I suppose that our lifestyle might not be everyone's "cup of tea," but we wouldn't have it any other way. All artists are a little bit crazy, but we truly love what we are doing. What has made our marriage last has been our basic "liking" of each other as well as the flexibility we have learned due to our interests in the arts. I'm afraid that both Bob and I would be frustrated and bored to tears if we were confined in a routine family environment and nine-to-five jobs. That would cause us to stagnate creatively. Our being unchallenged is probably the worst thing that could happen to our marriage. The wonderful salvation is that when Bob is down he can always pick up his guitar and we can head for a "picking party," or I can pick up my brush and create something beautiful out of chaos. That has helped us to survive and adjust to all the changes that come with life—being out of work (the creative job market is always mercurial), illness, the deaths and illnesses of parents, not to mention the financial obligations that come with two girls headed for college. Somehow, through everything, we still have faith that things will work out as long as we handle them together.

What's really nice is that with artist friends, Bob is Judy's husband; while with musicians, I am Bob's wife. Perhaps it is this give-and-take that makes having two or more artists in a family a lot of fun—even after twenty-one years.

Female artist
*Married twenty-six years
to a nonartist
Now divorced*

Q. *What do you think about artists and marriage? Or relationships?*

A. I'd like a chance, again, to make one work. I think I could be much better at it now than I was at twenty-three. I tried, but we never saw eye to eye. I suppose he thinks he tried, too.

I remember telling him, before we were married, never to treat art as a rival, because I was afraid he'd lose. He promised he wouldn't and then began to try to compete with my career as soon as the marriage vows were over. The minute he knew my mind was totally on painting, he would need a button sewn on his shirt, even though he had five other shirts he could have worn at that moment. I also suspect he could have used a needle and thread. He seemed capable at things he wanted to do.

Q. *Would it have worked better if you had been married to an artist?*

A. I don't know, but I think that now I'd understand an artist, writer, or musician better than a nonartist. I'd like that kind of relationship now, but don't think I could have handled it when I was younger—another ego to contend with.

Q. *Does an artist really need a spouse?*

A. Everyone needs someone. We aren't meant to be solitary creatures, at least I'm not. But as we get older, it becomes harder to adjust our life to another's. Art is all-consuming, 90 percent of the time, yet it's not enough sometimes.

Q. *What kind of man would you like in your life?*

A. Someone who stimulates my mind. Someone who understands the moods of an artist and takes the time to find out how to respond. I'd expect to do that for him, too; to find out what he needs and try to provide that. If two people were working together like that, how could they lose?

Male artist
*Married twenty years
Now divorced*

Q. *What do you think about marriage between two artists?*

A. I think a marriage or a relationship could survive, but the two artists involved must be flexible. They are two very special people. There are two egos to serve, both already spoken for, both already married to art.

Q. *Can you pinpoint anything that happened in your marriage that illustrates this?*

A. It was a matter of priorities. We didn't agree often. For instance, she wanted to clean up the place all the time and cleaning doesn't always go with my work. I think we used this kind of thing against one another.

Q. *Maybe as an excuse for the real underlying problem?*

A. Yes. The first commitment must be to one's own needs and each must realize this. When you are young, though, it is the wrong time to *think*. Reason should balance emotion if *possible*, but it doesn't always.

Female artist
*Married twenty-eight years
to a military man*

Q. *How did you adjust to marriage to a non-artist?*

A. I was an art major, not finished with schooling, when we married. After marriage there was a typical husband-wife relationship. We had a family and a fairly structured home life. My art career was submerged—that was not unusual for those times. My husband was not supportive of my art career. Then he went away on military duty for one year and the worm turned. When he came home, I had received peer approval and his opinion of my art no longer mattered to me. Now we function in two different worlds.

Q. *Is that good? Will the marriage survive?*

A. If it does, it will be because I decide there is no better situation for me. An artist isn't structured. His desire for that can't help but cause conflicts. I have had to comply by creating only from nine to five. I bargained to be wife, social secretary, mother. Then I changed. He didn't. Artists always evolve; [they] can't help it. I was not a jelled professional when I married and artists never stop evolving. In my case, my husband evolved, too—to one of the best in his field—but he has no interest in what I'm doing.

Q. *How could this be resolved?*

A. I've resolved it by recognizing he won't change; discussing it—very important—which helps me (he's trying, but not changing); and seeking approval among my fellow artists and keeping the most important part of my life separate from my marriage.

Q. *Why do you stay married?*

A. Twenty-eight years is a lot of common experience. Four beautiful children. I have a great deal of respect for, and I care enough for this man, to want to continue. The end of the story will come when my husband retires. If he makes me choose between sitting at home, rocking and holding his hand, and my career—he'll lose.

Q. *Did his military travel affect your career?*

A. Yes, but it wasn't all bad. We lived so many places that I had to constantly reestablish my career. That kept me competing and fighting, never complacent. That's good.

Male artist
*Married thirty years
to a nonartist*

Q. *What has your wife contributed to your career?*

A. Everything. And I do mean everything. She has, in a sense, given up her own creative life to support me.

Q. *Is that good?*

A. I think it has contributed to making our marriage work. I won't say that it wouldn't have worked anyway. She has enough art background that I think she might have been able to become an artist, but chose not to. She chose to be an artist through me.

Q. *Did you ask her to give up her life to yours?*

A. No. I don't think I did, but I know she

felt I wanted it that way. It has worked well. She is my agent and my best publicist. She also guards my time so that I can paint and produce. There are times, though, when I feel almost too much gratitude. It overshadows other feelings for her. Then I have to come back to the real reason we are together.

Q. *Do you want to say more about that? I sense that you are on very intimate ground.*

A. I'll say more. She has been very understanding of all my moods or we would not have made it. There have been times when I felt things for other women, felt they were more exciting than my wife, wished she would be more independent. I've had students and colleagues who stimulated my mind in a way that she did not always have time for, while raising my children and overseeing my career. I have sometimes wanted to just see what it would be like to live in a different way, but being a moral man, I never did. She tolerated my friendships with other women. I think she always knew they were only friendships, but I'm not sure I always did. The wife of a male artist who gets involved in workshops and shows has a lot to think about when her husband is away. I wonder if I'd have handled it as well if the shoe had been on the other foot.

Q. *What do you mean?*

A. Well, I've had some women artist friends who had the same problem with their husbands. They wanted more creative give-and-take, more time to smell the roses with another "kindred soul," which their husbands were not. I'm afraid I always identified with the guys — the husbands. I think I wanted freedom for myself that I was not willing to give to my wife. But I never took that freedom. And I'm sure I would not be the artist I am without her constant support.

Barbara Gresham
Artist
West Lafayette, Indiana

Q. *You have lived and worked in Pennsylvania, Kentucky, Georgia, Indiana — wherever your husband's life has taken you. How do you manage being wife, mother, and artist?*

A. From the very beginning, the dual roles of homemaker and artist have spawned strange combinations of humor and drama, of tension and smiles. I see the roles as two true parallel lines, one occasionally soaring on ahead of the other. The success of their coexistence depends solely on the bridges built from one to another. Bridges have to be built from both sides and traversed from both sides. The temptation for an artist is to allow her/himself to become totally engulfed by the creative experience. While that is a welcome state of being during the process of the work itself, it can become a problem when there are relationships to be maintained with those who see themselves as "outsiders." Therein is the key perception. It is the manner with which husbands and wives see themselves that is crucial.

It is easy to understand why the spouse of an artist may feel an isolated mate, because part of this being engulfed by the creative experience is a very private thing. However, so much of the experience is made richer by the sharing of it, by the building of bridges. Basic to this sharing is the simple desire to communicate. The creative effort involves a searching of the soul, a constant confrontation with success and failure, and an openness to new ideas. These are entities which are very personal in nature, and the sharing of them requires an openness which leaves one quite vulnerable. It is much easier to share the particulars of an office job, a business decision, a plant operation, or even decisions involving the comings and goings of children, than to open up one's soul and let someone else in on the painful drama and the rare elation of the creative search.

It is, perhaps, just as difficult to be on the receiving end. When a fellow human being lays open his innermost struggles, most people are quite uneasy, are repelled by the intensity of the communication. The spouse of an artist has to face this intensity with regularity. There are times when the creative search brings an agony of silence more difficult to bridge than the spoken frustration. Besides the frustrations within the work itself, artists face constant criticism from media critics and amateur critics alike, constant fluctuations and fickleness on the part of museums, galleries, and the buying public. In short, it is an explosive, unsteady affair. Perhaps some marriages just aren't up to the added strain.

With an attitude of dedication, however, these seemingly negative facets of an artist's life could be turned into positive opportunities to enrich and deepen all communication between artist and mate. It is much more difficult for the marriage to get by on shallow commitments, and perhaps that is really a good thing. The world through the artist's eye is full of surprises, unique juxtapositions, and often a mysterious sense of *déjà vu*. A marriage that determines itself sound enough to share those things has depth and the elasticity for change. It truly is not a threat; it is an opportunity for a deeper, more whole marriage. If the crucial bridges of trust and sharing are established on this profound level, the bridges of a more particular nature seem to span themselves. If there are children involved, there is the usual sharing of responsibility that goes along with both marriage partners working. The difference is the erratic schedule of an artist and the depth of involvement. As an artist-mother I can only present that particular role with the negatives and positives that pertain to it. Most are positives, thank goodness!

Q. *How about your children—what do they think of your life?*

A. I once heard of an interview with a famous musician in which he was asked if he minded the "unusualness" of his upbringing. When he was a child his mother spent four hours a day practicing the cello while he played quietly at her feet. For all he knew, all mothers did that! My children may not choose to be artists, but since my first child was two years old, I have spent four or more hours a day painting. So, that is "normal" to my children. What is a real bonus is that the creative experience, the seeking and finding of one's own answers, the looking at the world visually and conceptually in a unique way, is also normal to them. The struggle of success and failure and the courage to be alone is right there in their own house, and I cannot help but believe that they will be stronger, yet more sensitive, human beings because of it.

The bridge that I build from the "artist's line" to the "others' line" must be one that invites my children to cross. Although much of my work I must do alone, many times I've invited them to paint with me or to go sit together in the woods to "see what we can see."

My children are no strangers to art exhibits, be it outdoor fairs or museums; that's another little bonus. Viewing exhibits in which there is one of Mom's paintings has become "old hat." So has viewing exhibits from which Mom's paintings have been rejected! The whole family shares the successes and the failures. Sometimes with extreme effort I have to lay aside the defeats and the victories (for either will dictate a narrow pathway) and continue the search from my own viewpoint. This is a particular dilemma which forces the visual artist to embrace the whole of life almost daily. To invite children into this world, in a way, forces them to embrace the whole of life, too. To keep the experience from becoming too overpowering, there must remain in the forefront the simple truth that personal victories and defeats are rather meaningless unless they are shared. As one artist friend reminded me, "Remember, art comes from life. Life does not come from art." Build your bridges.

Q. *Your approach to life is great and I'm sure your children love it, but how do you and your husband keep your equilibrium?*

A. The balancing act of artist-homemaker is rather like the old jokes about "the good news and the bad news." The good news is that it isn't a nine-to-five job, so I can be home when my children get off the school bus, I can plan corresponding vacation time with my husband, and, of course, I save so much gasoline, etc., not driving to work because I can work at home. The bad news is that it's difficult to explain to some others that it is still a job, that one must work regularly and in

depth. It is also difficult to find true friends who will accept one's dedication to one's work without considering it a personal affront. Maybe that is why so many "arty types" stick together! The balancing act continues with volunteer work one is expected to do, because, after all, it isn't as if painting is a job—legitimate, that is. Also, the bad news is that if I hear, "What a nice hobby" at one more party, I might scream!

The good news is, it is all worth it. It is an approach to life which demands that I constantly examine my soul and the soul of life itself. It is a way of life which says that I will never feel like the lyrics of the song that Peggy Lee sings, "Is that all there is?" It is a way of living that has taught me that I will change in the way I see things, the way I react to things. I don't expect to stay the same. Therefore, I can accept more readily change in my husband and my children. The *fear* of change for us all is lessened.

There are a few frivolous things with which we have built bridges. My husband was once a dye chemist and the differences in the color vocabulary of a chemist and an artist proved rather amusing. I have a deep appreciation for working neutral colors; to him they are just "dirty." To him it is a red-brown; to me it is burnt sienna. The little dog I had for fifteen years carefully walked around all pieces of paper when I was painting (I paint on the floor), but went charging through and over anything when I wasn't. Even she was part of the bridge-building.

One important observation about parallel lines is that, by definition, they never really converge. If two straight lines do cross each other, they must then go in different directions. Two parallel lines with bridges can go on into infinity.

Gallery

"Todd, Sailing Forever," Edna Wagner Piersol, 30 x 30 inches, watercolor on tissue paper coated with wax.

This is a posthumous portrait of a young man who fought cancer from 17 to 20 years of age and then lost the battle. His mother asked me to do his portrait in such a way that he spend forever doing his favorite thing in life — sailing. I never knew Todd but worked from fifty or so photos of him from childhood on. When it was time to paint in the blue jeans, I felt Todd would want me to stop, not paint them — let his figure fade away. I feared that would affect his mother badly, but she allowed me to stop, with tears in her eyes. Portrait work is demanding beyond description, but it's very rewarding to work so closely with people to produce what they want and need. Later this picture appealed so much to another woman in another part of the country that she bought a photographic copy of it from me. Before she knew the title she murmured, "It looks just like my boys, forever young, forever sailing."

This color gallery has two sections. The first section contains a critique of paintings that will help to show any struggling artist in what direction to struggle—to use effort instead of just expend it.

As you go through the critique, I'm sure you will find many suggestions that speak directly to you and your problems almost as though these were critiques of your work instead of another artist's. Each critique revolves around answering the four questions to analyze the quality of a painting discussed on pages 30-32. There are several places where my comments refer to something that the artist has told me in her unpublished cover letter. Those comments are self-explanatory and will show you how professionally she analyzed her own work but then needed a second opinion.

The second section contains works of art by the artists who have shared their thoughts with you in the book. These paintings will show you how other artists have put into practice the principles we've discussed in both creating and marketing their work.

Critiquing Your Own Work

As I pointed out in Chapter 3, it's important to learn how to be your own best critic because the key to living by your brush alone is producing absolutely the best work you're capable of. Everything else is secondary to that.

All you have to do is learn how to use the four questions discussed earlier:
- Does the painting check out by the four-quarter method?
- Does it have a warm or cool dominance?
- Does it contain light, medium, and dark values?
- Where does the lightest light meet the darkest dark?

To help you see how to use those four questions, let's take a look at a critique I did for a very specialized artist. The four questions apply to any kind of painting so these comments will be helpful reading no matter what your specialty.

A couple of years ago Dawn Weimer, an artist from Fort Collins, Colorado, began an indepth analysis of her art career. One of her decisions, among many at that time, was to seek some help from me after reading an earlier edition of this book. She also studied books by other artists.

Since then, Weimer has achieved magnificent results as you will see in her dog portraits on page 111. Her portraits of all kinds of animals have now started her on the road to fame. Here is an excerpt from a recent letter that shows the kind of interest from the buying public all of her efforts have produced:

Dear Edna,

Please forgive the little delay in sending these materials to you, but I had a deadline on a dog portrait and I had to get it completed. Now that she is finished I can take some time to get this material to you as the six other portraits waiting for me in the studio do not have pressing deadlines.

Your critiques and your first book have been very helpful to me. You helped me to have courage. I needed to begin to take myself seriously and help others do the same, like friends who think since you 'work at home' they can call and keep you on the phone for two hours at a time! Also, I am beginning to stand up for my work; and when someone refers to my 'hobby,' I can politely remind them that it is my business.

Most of these critiques were done two years before the work Weimer is producing now. The critiqued paintings needed some help (doesn't every painting, in the eyes of its creator?) but were already quite good and some of them have been sold without changes, which only goes to show you that everyone has a different opinion of art. Learn to have faith in your work even if it does, at times, need criticism.

Strengths: The drawing is very good and the painting has good contrasts (but they aren't all placed correctly).

Weaknesses: If you check the design by the four-quarter method, you'll see that three of the four quadrants need help. The upper-right quadrant is fine, but the two lower quarters have very strong diagonal lines where lights meet dark, leading the viewer's eye out of the picture. The highlighted leaf in the upper left helps balance the contrasts on the chipmunk's head, but it should point at the chipmunk. A little more highlight added to a branch above the chipmunk and some of the branches in the lower left could be used to create a sunburst effect and draw attention to the star of the show—the chipmunk.

Because the chipmunk is soft and warm, it needs to be played against something hard and cool. Maybe the rocks and the branch edges in the area close to the chipmunk could be painted with harder edges. For a strong interest grabber, the artist could make the chipmunk's eye even brighter.

"In the Thick of It," Dawn Weimer, 22 x 28 inches, acrylic.

Strengths: This is a good painting, displaying what I call "harmony of marks." It looks as if the artist loved making every brushstroke and knew exactly why she placed it where it is. The value contrasts are good and the whites form a pattern. The artist created a good center of interest in the lower left of the painting, with strong whites against darks. A path of yellow leads up to the large bush at the upper right, and the bush is *not* in the center of a quadrant, which would make the composition too stagnant.

Weaknesses: In the lower left quadrant the line created by the back of the goose's neck is almost exactly in the center of the quadrant. It would have looked better slightly off center.

"Lake Island Repose, Canada Geese," Dawn Weimer, 22 x 28 inches, acrylic.

109

"Outfoxed?" Dawn Weimer, 10 x 16 inches, acrylic.

Strengths: Although the tree is rather centered, I like it—its angle adds a movement to the painting that is good. The crisp white edges of snow on the fallen log and pine branches make me smell the cold day, and the snow shadows are created with lovely mauve grays.

Weaknesses: The big problem with this painting is improper use of contrasts. Contrast should be used to draw attention to the center of interest, yet the ptarmigan is so well hidden in the bushes at the base of the tree that a viewer probably wouldn't even see it. The ptarmigan, an important supporting player to the fox, should be peeking out at the fox on the other side of the tree so that its dark red head would show up as a silhouette against the snow.

Overall, the painting has too many areas of mild contrast that give the viewer no idea where to look. I'd subdue the light areas in the upper left and all the whites (except the areas of snow I mentioned and those on the fox and in the center area) to spotlight the fox and ptarmigan. Adding a very light glaze of the mauve grays to the light and white areas would do the trick.

"Early Lessons," Dawn Weimer, 15 x 30 inches, acrylic.

Strengths: This painting has good color and does a good job of conveying a wilderness feeling.

Weaknesses: Think what would happen if this painting were cropped on the right, just beyond the little bear, cutting out the trees in the upper right quadrant. That would eliminate the feeling that there is a hole in the middle of this painting. Breaking up the diagonal line of white water against a dark background with lost-and-found edges in the rocks along the bank would also help create a strong center of interest right on the three bears.

"Jock," Dawn Weimer, 16 x 20 inches, acrylic.

"Rocky & Kalee," Dawn Weimer, 12 x 16 inches, acrylic.

"Jock" is a marvelous rendition of a black Labrador using a very popular technique of no background, just the dog's head in white space. The silhouette dominates and is the center of interest because of the strong contrast of dark against light. But if the dog's features had not been skillfully handled, the shape of the head could have totally dominated — not his personality. Compare that to "Rocky & Kalee," which Weimer painted two years later. The areas of strong contrast are inside the dog's faces, allowing the personality of each dog to become the center of interest. The Dalmations painting, which has been accepted as the future cover for a national breeder's magazine, shows the tremendous strides Weimer made in just a couple of years. In fact, she has now progressed so far beyond her early student status, I'm grateful she allowed her lessons to be published for others' benefit.

"Kimono," Barbara Gresham, 24 x 37 inches, collage of watercolor, acrylic, rice paper, found paper.

This is the painting we critiqued on page 32 using the four-quarter method. You can see now that it also checks out well using the other three questions.

"At the End Even the Sky Turns to Red," Claire Justine, 15 x 20 inches, collage.

Pictures of "real things" are more understandable than abstracts to viewers who aren't educated in art, so Justine combines that appeal with good solid composition and color use to create collages that can be appreciated by both the novice and the seasoned viewer.

"Deer Crossing—White Tails," Randy McGovern, 16 x 20 inches, oil.

Hiding small creatures in his work has become a sort of trademark for McGovern and is just the kind of thing the public loves. This painting has eight creatures hidden in it.

"The Galleria," Edna Wagner Piersol, 30 x 40 inches, watercolor.

This is another of the paintings I did for the mayor of Louisville. Compare it to the one on page 32, and you'll see that capturing an entire city requires a lot of variety in your painting. Never overlook public places when seeking commissions.

"Sharon," Joan Coate Milsom, 48 x 60 inches, oil.

This strong figure painting is the kind of work that might interest a good decorator or gallery owner. It would also make a fine piece for a corporate collection, unless that particular organization had a restriction against displaying nudes in its buildings.

"Grandma Dragon," Keets Rivers, 13 x 7 x 9 inches, terra cotta.

All artists do not live by their *brushes* alone. Anyone able to create whimsy in clay as well as Keets Rivers has a ready market.

"Landscape Phenomena," Kathryn Witte, 30 x 40 inches, oil on canvas.

Rich deep colors attract the viewer. Most of Witte's paintings are abstract but they give such deep hints of subject that the paintings become "all things to all people." Witte says that at an outdoor show, she features just one or two paintings like this at a time, allowing the full impact to hit the viewer, and then puts up a new painting in an hour or two.

"Mysteries of the Mind," Aline Barker, 30 x 22 inches, mixed waterbased media.

Aline Barker proves again and again that an artist can explore her own mind and still please the buying public. The intriguing color patterns engage the eye and cause the viewer to sense all kinds of shapes—each person seeing something different, yet pleasing. That helps sell a painting.

"Beach Find," Autry Dye, 24 x 40 inches, watercolor.

Autry Dye has used "Beach Find," which was featured in a book about Florida artists, as promotional material several times—which is what you should do when you have a very good piece. Don't just sell it and forget it. Keep the reproduction rights and good slides so you can use it whenever you like.

"Grey Aspens," Charles Pitcher, 22 x 30 inches, watercolor.

An artist must not make the mistake of trying to copy nature in order to be popular. It won't work. Good painting like Pitcher's trees will usually win a prospective buyer away from realism for its own sake, which can be very dull.

"Western Landscape," Jerry Caplan, 27 x 16 x 6 inches, terra cotta and acrylic.

This work gives you the illusion of being able to look deep into it, a feeling of space and freedom, very western, very spacious with the sky contained. When you can give a viewer that kind of release from his cramped life, you have created great appeal. As an artist, when you have given someone solace, you have created a market.

"Canyon Rim," Marge Alderson, 28 x 36 inches, mixed media.

This is a painting with a powerful hint of many kinds of subject matter just below the surface. When an artist learns to use composition, that artist has created a tool for entering the viewer's subconscious. What better way to create a sale? This is composition at its best.

"Death & Resurrection," Edna Wagner Piersol, 36 x 28 inches, watercolor.

This kind of painting is often popular with decorators but each decorator has at least one specialty, so do some research before you approach any decorator.

Photo by Jack Collins, Smyrna, Georgia

"Covered Bridge," J. Price Wiesman, 15 x 25 inches, acrylic. From the collection of Logan Construction Company.

J. Price Wiesman did this painting on commission, but liked it so much that she bartered with the owner: rather than pay her for the painting, he printed materials featuring the painting for Wiesman to use in promoting her work.

Conclusion

"Memories," Edna Wagner Piersol, 30 x 40 inches, watercolor.

In conclusion, I would like to share with you my philosophy of teaching painting and sharing ideas that has been with me throughout my professional life. *If you are going to become better at painting than I am — I might as well help you as much as I can and then take part in your glory.*

You've heard my views and those of other artists, now take a moment to *write down on paper* what you want from your life and then go after it. Living by your brush alone is the most excitingly creative venture I can imagine — creating a *life*, not just a painting or two.

Farewell, happy painting and, most of all, happy living.

This painting invokes just that — memories — in anyone who looks at it. The subject was a real corner of a kitchen I once had, and still miss, painted when I knew I would soon leave it behind. Perhaps that feeling comes across to the viewer but an artist must watch sentimentality when painting this way, even though many buyers like it. Much better to rely strongly on composition and contrast power in painting (as I hope I have) than mere sentimentality. Buyers respond even more strongly to composition than to sentimentality even though they don't realize it.

Index